PRAISE FOR AGENDA

Ed Horak's book Agenda *presents a concise treatise on the "Politics of Crisis" and socialism, which presents a clear and present danger to all of us. Agenda reveals, with facts and figures, the Socialist agenda for America, and how it is the antithesis of the two greatest authoritative works in history, the Bible and the US Constitution. This book is a warning and a great read that should be required reading for every citizen, if not in every church and classroom in America!*

BILL BRUBAKER, NAVY CAPTAIN
(RETIRED), SEATTLE, WA

Recently, I had the opportunity to read Ed Horak's latest book, Agenda, *and was blown away by the ease and candor with which he connects the dots and brings light to the current political environment and how it impacts each of us. This is a must read!*

FRANK ESPINOZA, CLIMACO
CONSULTING LLC, SEATTLE, WA

To be ignorant of what is going on in the world is one thing; to remain ignorant is inexcusable. If you are like me, [and you] watch the politicians and mainstream media perpetrate mass hysteria about global warming, COVID-19, etc., this book will enlighten you and give you the right perspective of the cause and the cure to this hysteria. Agenda is easy to understand and paints a picture that exposes the tyranny of the leftist Big Government and a One World Order mandate. When you know the Truth, the truth will make you free.

REV. GERRI DI SOMMA FOUNDER,
PRESIDENT, AND SENIOR MINISTER, CARMEL
GLOBAL MINISTRIES INC, UK/USA

"*Agenda is a thought-provoking book that needs to be part of the material you consider when you are forming your opinions—or even the decisions you may have to make for your family. Author Ed Horak provides a very readable and understandable presentation of many issues so pressing in our nation, culture, and world.*"

KEITH HERSHEY, MUTUAL FAITH MINISTRIES
INTERNATIONAL, MISSION HILLS, CALIFORNIA

If you want to find out the state of the world today, and possibly where we will end up tomorrow without divine intervention, I encourage you to read this book.

Author Ed lays an easy-to-read yet solid historical background of grand themes such as communism, and socialism and the church. He progressively introduces more current themes, such as globalism, and population control, that adversely affect our lives today. The work is a mini thesis of well-researched facts of how the mind of man operating without the wisdom of God has systematically made our world an increasingly intolerable place in which to live. I like the systematic and clear writing style that Ed adopts, making the reader want to get to the next chapter. Agenda *is a wake-up call to those who want to know how the systematic dismantling of God-ordained society has progressed into the potential setup of a one-world government. Ed ends with what we can and should do as we are summoned by God to pray for this generation. Well done, Ed, a great read.*

TOM INGLIS, SENIOR PASTOR, SYDNEY LIFE CHURCH, AUSTRALIA; PRESIDENT, PSALMODY INTERNATIONAL

Is it possible that the turmoil we are witnessing in the world today can be the result of a well-crafted conspiracy that began decades ago? Are socialism, climate change, and globalism all part of a plan to bring about a utopian "one-world government"? Ed Horak carefully and thoughtfully reveals what we are facing today and why Christians need to be aware of the deceptive agenda to rob us of our liberties. What does the Bible have to say about it? In a simple, yet thorough narrative, Ed will reveal the truth behind the current agenda on the world stage. If you are wondering what on earth is going on, I highly recommend Ed's book Agenda *to bring clarity.*

ANDREW THORNE, BROKER, ARE COMMERCIAL AND RESIDENTIAL REAL ESTATE, CALIFORNIA

"Ed's latest book, Agenda, *is a must read for anyone interested in knowing the truth about the current events impacting our society. He clearly exposes the dangers of socialism, which is gaining popularity amongst millennials and on college campuses across America. President Trump's policy of nationalism is in direct opposition to the globalism policy of the liberal left, which is why they must see him fail—at any cost. Ed drills down and reveals the truth behind the fear-driven COVID-19 pandemic, with its hidden agenda of population control and the loss of personal liberty. Ed masterfully deals with the church's role in modern America and gives great insight into the conflict with secular humanism. Do we really have freedom of religion in the United States?"*

DR. HENRY WOLMARANS, SENIOR PASTOR, PROMISE CHURCH, ESCONDIDO, CALIFORNIA

AGENDA

SOCIALISM IN THE WEST

WHAT IS REALLY GOING ON?

EDMUND H. HORAK

River Publishing

AGENDA

FIRST EDITION

Copyright © 2020 Edmund H Horak

All rights reserved. No part of this book may be reproduced in any form or by any electronic or mechanical means, including information storage and retrieval systems, without permission in writing from the publisher, except by a reviewer who may quote brief passages in a review.

Trademarked names appear throughout this book. The Author recognizes all registered trademarks and service marks mentioned in the text.

The internet addresses listed in the text were accurate at the time of publication. The inclusion of a website does not include an endorsement by the author and does not guarantee the accuracy of the information presented at these sites.

Every attempt has been made to trace accurate ownership of copyrighted material in this book. Errors or omissions will be corrected in subsequent editions, provided that notification is sent to the publisher.

Unless otherwise indicated, Scripture quotations are taken from the New King James Version. Copyright ©1979, 1980, 1982 by Thomas Nelson Inc. Used with permission. All rights reserved.

Scripture quotations marked ESV are taken from The Holy Bible, English Standard Version. ESV® Text Edition: 2016. Copyright © 2001 by Crossway Bibles, a publishing ministry of Good News Publishers.

Scriptures marked KJV are taken from the Holy Bible, King James Version (public domain).

Scripture quotations marked NIV are taken from the New International Version (NIV) Holy Bible, New International Version®, NIV® Copyright ©1973, 1978, 1984, 2011 by Biblica, Inc.® Used by permission. All rights reserved worldwide.

ISBN 978-1-64970-823-6

Printed in the United States of America

To my dear wife and mother of our children, Sue. Thank you all for your love, support, and commitment to truth and freedom. May God's blessing be upon our children—Janine, Matthew, Ben, and daughter-in-love, Angela—and grandchildren to a thousand generations.

CONTENTS

Foreword xi

1 **Agenda** 1
   Everybody Has One

2 **Liberals, Leftists, and More** 9
   The Collective versus the Individual

3 **Globalism Defined, and How It Connects with Socialism** 19
   A New World Order?

4 **Socialism in the United States** 39
   Seriously?

5 **What Did George Orwell Say about Facebook and YouTube?** 49
   Nothing?

6 **The Rise of Socialism among Millennials** 59
   Is the Social Justice Emphasis Legitimate?

7 **Church and State Separation/Secular Humanism/Socialism** 71
   Freedom *of* Religion or Freedom *from* Religion?

8 **Population-Growth Control** 81
   What Has This to Do with Socialism?

9 **The Coronavirus 2019/2020 Event** 93
   Connecting the Dots

10 **Climate Change** 123
   Things Are Hotting Up

| 11 | **What Is the Agenda behind the Agenda?** | 137 |

Green Is the New Red

| 12 | **Was Jesus a Socialist?** | 145 |

The True and the False Gospel

| 13 | **Did the Early Church Practice a Form of Socialism?** | 159 |

Community Living Is the Answer . . . or Is It?

| 14 | **Kingdom Principles of *True* Prosperity** | 165 |

God's Plan All Along

| 15 | **Why Does All This Matter?** | 169 |

And What to Do

Addendum 1: Know Your Rights 174

The First Ten Amendments to the US Constitution

Addendum 2: Vaccines 177

Besides Health, Is There an Agenda Here?

Addendum 3: Who Are "They"? 188

Globalist World Influencers and Their Socialist Cohorts

About the Author 193

FOREWORD

DR. RODNEY HOWARD-BROWNE

Because I travel about forty-six weeks of the year and have held weekly meetings in cities across North America and in eighty-five nations worldwide, I clearly see and deeply understand the great value behind this book, *Agenda*.

Ed and I are from South Africa. Both of us have seen horrific atrocities committed against men, women, and children. Many of these brutal crimes were committed in

FOREWORD

the name of "justice." Justice was not served; it was never at the heart of the matter. Cruel agendas and selfish gains are what fuel and feed much of the corruption around the globe.

Ed Horak does a phenomenal job in *Agenda*. The title is perfect, and the material is absolutely pertinent for the times in which we are living. Hosea 4:6 reads, "My people are destroyed for lack of knowledge." Ed presents truth and facts in a well-organized fashion, precept upon precept and line upon line.

Sadly, much of what is published as news, whether in the newspapers or on the networks, is filled with lies, misinformation, and propaganda. People are making wrong decisions based on wrong information. The only way an educated and wise decision can be made is when sound, solid, and truthful information is conveyed.

Deceptive tactics are used every day to control the masses. This book will help unleash the truth and reveal the heart of the matter. "Ye shall know them by their fruits. Do men gather grapes of thorns, or figs of thistles? Even so every good tree bringeth forth good fruit; but a corrupt tree bringeth forth evil fruit. A good tree cannot bring forth evil fruit, neither can a corrupt tree bring forth good fruit. Every tree that bringeth not forth good fruit is hewn down, and cast into the fire. Wherefore by their fruits ye shall know them" (Matthew 7:16–20 KJV).

In this book, you will learn the importance of digging a little deeper, following the money, getting to the root of the issue, and being proactive.

FOREWORD

You will tremendously benefit from *Agenda*, as it not only shines the light on the problem, but it offers the solution. You may find yourself making new decisions based on new and true information. "And ye shall know the truth, and the truth shall make you free" (John 8:32 KJV). May you get ready to be challenged, be inspired, and most important, make a difference!

DR. RODNEY HOWARD-BROWNE, PASTOR/AUTHOR,
REVIVAL MINISTRIES INTERNATIONAL, TAMPA, FLORIDA

1

AGENDA

EVERYBODY HAS ONE

> *There are many plans in a man's heart,*
> *Nevertheless the LORD's counsel [purpose or*
> *agenda]—that will stand.*
>
> —PROVERBS 19:21

Politicians, preachers, socialists, and capitalists all have an agenda. Kids and teenagers too. Some are more sophisticated than others: from the kid throwing a tantrum to get something that his parents have forbidden to the politician who takes advantage of a crisis to slip in aspects to a bill that normally wouldn't pass in calmer times. See, I have already started on my agenda, which is to disrupt your normal pattern of thinking and hopefully cause you to see things that happen around us today from a different perspective.

As a disclaimer, I am a "regular" person doing research on the internet, reading articles and books, talking to people around me, and listening to podcasts, radio, and, yes, even some news clips put out by the media. This opinion piece that I have written is therefore a digest of what has made sense to me. It is not an academic treatise that claims to be definitive, with all the necessities of such an approach. If you can live with that, then continue reading.

I also know in part and communicate in part (see 1 Corinthians 13:9). That is true of everyone, including you, and even "experts" in the field of your interest.

To begin, you may ask me, "Surely you are not saying that population control, climate change, and COVID-19 are connected somehow to socialism?"

Yes, I am.

I live in the Seattle area in the northwestern United States and have come to see a web or latticework of regulations that impact every aspect of life, from religion to food. I believe the patterns and latest trends here are largely replicated across the USA and worldwide, at least in what may be called modern economies.

These regulations, whether at a local, state, or national level, have often been imposed on us in a top-down manner, where supposed informed consent in the political process has been bypassed by leaders who often issue directives to advance their ideological agenda.

AGENDA

Of course, we need such regulations as speed limits and building codes for safety purposes, but when your constitutional rights are trampled on in the name of some top-down ruling, backed not by sound science but by agenda-driven "science," things get tricky.

Top-down rule (and control) has existed throughout history and is most often enacted by law and enforced ultimately with weaponry owned or controlled only by those in authority.

In cases of bad law and dictatorial control, the general populace must put up with everything that gets handed down by authorities, unless they rise in rebellion, which often costs them their freedom and/or lives.

In America at least, there has an ongoing experiment with a representative democracy within a constitutional republic that has pushed back on the control ruling "elites" have historically exerted over the people.

Ratified on July 4, 1776, the US Declaration of Independence from British monarchical rule began:

> We hold these truths to be self-evident, that all men are created equal, that they are endowed by their Creator with certain unalienable Rights, that among these are Life, Liberty and the pursuit of Happiness.

Today as at any time in US history, if you are an officer of any sort at any level of service in the republic, you swear to defend the Constitution against enemies foreign and domestic. Implicit in your service is an acknowledgment that there is an indispensable spiritual or moral component to American society and culture. The rights with which we are endowed come from the "Creator," whom we know from the Bible to be a moral person, and not some vague force that can be ignored at will.

We are ultimately accountable to the giver of these "unalienable Rights." Anyone who rules outside the constraints of the Constitution must be held to account, and anyone who interacts unjustly with his or her fellow man is also accountable to the Creator. The preamble to the Constitution is not there to fill up space on paper. It is foundational to what follows.

These rights are not conferred on citizens by human consensus, political process, and agreement alone. When a nation acknowledges that it is "under God," as attested in the Pledge of Allegiance to the Flag of the United States of America, it invites His wisdom and divine perspective to enable its citizens to face the challenges of modern society. We prosper, not by our efforts alone, but with God's help. The founding fathers of the US understood the need for God's transcendence, that society must have a moral underpinning. Our universe is not merely natural; it is spiritual too.

In God's cosmos, everything serves a purpose. If His purposes (and ways) are ignored or distorted, a tension develops that no amount of government law or systemic change can solve. Only God can solve this shortcoming, through His salvation.

Socialists who exclude God from their understanding of life are left to their own devices.

Socialism is rooted in Karl Marx's atheism, where the very existence of God is denied and thus His right to guide our affairs on this earth. In this ideology humans are the masters of their universe. In effect, socialism becomes man's attempt to "save" himself. So far, history has shown that man has not done such a great job at saving himself. We will see that in our case studies of socialist societies in the twentieth century in a later chapter.

A quick word about the word *agenda*. Everyone has an agenda based on their worldview or comprehensive framework of ideas and attitudes through which the world is to be understood.

My agenda is to shine some light in the darkness as I see it. My worldview stems from my unique life journey, which includes a Judeo-Christian point of view. I filter what I experience and understand through a grid of my understanding of God and His purposes. Before I came to know God through Jesus, I used to be a typically arrogant and foolishly inexperienced student at a liberal/leftist university. As I grew in the faith and "detoxed" from the indoctrination I had received at university, my mind was renewed, as the Bible teaches (see Romans 12:1–2). My worldview changed, and so did I. I began to see the big picture so much better, and I understood more about where people were coming from, that is, their agenda.

Lovers of truth are always open to hearing the other party out, so tread on and hear me out.

AGENDA

I define an *agenda* as:

1. a list of things to be considered or done
2. an underlying plan or program
3. a political and/or ideological stance

When advancing an agenda, in the second sense, you must believe that what you are doing is the "right" thing to do. Otherwise, why do anything at all? Doing anything else would therefore be "wrong."

Facts, data, science, reason, and sometimes inspiration should be the foundation of any agenda. I contend that it is naive to think that things such as ideology, greed, and selfish profiteering do not factor into the pursuit of "science." Science is a tainted pursuit, as it is performed by scientists, each with his or her own shortcomings and, yes, agenda.

Scientific research, even with all its methodologies, peer reviews, and its consequent practical application, falls short of perfection. First, what we know today will change tomorrow, and second, every scientist (and his or her funders) has a worldview and an agenda.

Are we doomed to put up with what we get, or can progress be made with liberal helpings of humility and strong doses of honesty and transparency? I think progress *can* be made. In fact, hugely beneficial advances have already been made through science (medicine, food production, communications, etc.). Yet in the end, godly character remains a key foundation of truth, and scientific practice cannot and

AGENDA

should not be divorced from the pursuit of truth.

A heads-up: some of what you will read in this book will fall into what some call "conspiracy theory." By the way, this term may well have been promoted by the CIA as derogatory, back in the day when people began to question the Warren Commission's findings on the assassination of JFK. Since that time, skeptics of all things official have consistently been branded as "conspiracy theorists," and their views encouraged to be dismissed. When you realize that no one is agenda-free, even those in control of branding others as "conspiracy theorists," you have started to see things more clearly.

In our day, we have rediscovered that sunlight, once feared, is good for you. So are fresh air and a healthy immune system, free from the fear and stress that lockdowns help produce. Good, wholesome, nutrient-rich food is good too.

There is a connection to all this and socialism.

So, let the light shine in.

2

LIBERALS, LEFTISTS, AND MORE

THE COLLECTIVE VERSUS THE INDIVIDUAL

A wise man's heart inclines him to the right, but a fool's heart to the left.

—ECCLESIASTES 10:2 (ESV)

Now, that is controversial, but it need not be.

Most people desire the same things in life: freedom, opportunities for prosperity, minimized suffering, peace, healthy children, and crime-free streets. I guess this kind of society might be some version of heaven on earth. Without getting too theological at this point, these goals are high indeed, but they need God's intervention and cannot be truly and lastingly achieved without His help. Nevertheless, men and women still try to create utopia in the here and now, whether they be liberals on the left, or conservatives on the right.

Liberals tend to focus on the role of government action and centralized control to ensure equal opportunity and equality for all. They believe government is the key agency that will alleviate social ills and protect civil liberties and basic human rights so that no one in need is without help. It is a top-down approach.

Conservatives emphasize personal responsibility, limited government, and free markets to promote opportunity. Government should only provide the freedom necessary for the individual to pursue his or her own goals. Government, the conservative asserts, should be limited to providing a playing field of empowerment of individuals to solve their own problems and promote themselves. It is more of a bottom-up approach.

Enter *leftists*, or *progressives*, who are also liberals, but not of the traditional stripe. Leftists take things further than your conventional liberal, using universities as a key example of modern trends. Leftists exalt personal feelings over traditionally reliable reason. Diverse debate is often shut down in the name of protecting so-called diversity. Those whose opinions differ from theirs are labeled as "hate speech–mongers," "racists," and "bigots." Racism is supposedly "systemic," or built into the machinery of society now more than ever. White privilege as represented by male conservative Protestant types is something that must be attacked. Further, leftists rant about gender issues as if they are one of the greatest threats to human existence.

These and other issues are to be systematically deconstructed because basic Western, and particularly, American values are bad compared to some sort of leftist utopia that has yet to be created despite a century and a half of trying. Progressive policies simply have not delivered for the people.

REGARDING FREE SPEECH, THE PRESS, AND LEFTISTS

The Soviet broadsheet newspaper, ironically called *Pravda*, or "Truth," was the official communications organ of the Communist Party in the USSR between 1912 and 1991. It served as part of the government propaganda arm, yet most Soviet citizens were not fooled by their spin media.

Today, many US citizens tend to believe the "mainstream media" (MSM)—CNN, NBC, ABC, Fox, MSNBC, the *New York Times*, the *Washington Post*, and so on—to be reliable sources of news. Seemingly blind to the biases or agendas promoted by these outlets, large swaths of the populace dutifully tune in daily to what may often be called "left-leaning" or even "fake" news. Some have even called the narrative pushed by these outlets "public participation management." Facts, science, and data are all filtered through a grid where clear objectivity is lost in the slanted, agenda-driven rhetoric. Facts are "processed," or "spun" so that they never get in the way of a good story or the narrative being pushed. Talking heads spout "talking points," and no real reporting is done. Ideology and ratings rule, being good for business and for advancing the agenda. Strict neutrality and journalistic ethics go out the window. More and more, mainstream media journalists are no longer honest reporters but propaganda hacks advancing a leftist/socialist agenda.

Joe Citizen is now actively steered by editors in a political direction. These media manipulators argue that they have a role to play in making society better, more just, fair, and so on. Of course, they define what is better from a moral high ground they have claimed for themselves. Distortion and spin are the order of the day; some information is often underplayed or underreported.

Calling out fake news for what it is, is not a disservice or an attack on the freedom of the press. Journalists cannot enjoy a free pass to be disingenuous. They are not free to promote a sociopolitical agenda of their liking at the expense of other points of view. Modern democratic society values honest debate, not a leftist agenda–driven control of the flow of information.

Even internet giants such as Google, Facebook, and YouTube bury certain reporting that they deem not to meet their platforms' standards. Of course, they will argue that their algorithms are intended simply to effect a fair and just policy of political correctness. Yet when you step back, you see that this amounts to negative censorship. The individual is denied the opportunity to decide for himself or herself. If something is true, it will stand up to scrutiny where clear-thinking, reasonable people who display true tolerance will examine matters without being told what to believe and what not to believe. Of course, you must teach people growing up *how* to be clear thinkers, not *what* to think.

The traditional liberal sees the extensive use of the levers of power through government as a key tool in alleviating socioeconomic ills. But the more modern liberal—today's more radical leftist—seeks more to dismantle or deconstruct society in classic Marxist fashion. Leftists attack the integrity of the American Constitution as they label anyone in opposition as racist, misogynistic, homophobic, or bigoted. The conventional liberal solution is focused on education and exposure to their more "enlightened" ideas; however, the leftists of today are more likely to shout you down with their megaphones.

WHAT ABOUT LIBERTARIANS?

Libertarians claim to be a distinct group who take man's desire for freedom to greater lengths than do others. Liberty is maximized in the political sphere through a push for autonomy, freedom of choice, voluntary association, and individual judgment. Libertarians are intensely skeptical of government power and advocate limited state welfare programs. At the far-left end of the political spectrum, libertarians look a lot like anarchists, who are strongly opposed to most if not all authority. These extremists espouse free association versus any form of imposed hierarchical authority structures. They may even resort to either revolutionary or evolutionary means to achieve their ends.

Antifa groups in the United States include anarchists as well as socialists and communists, and when given the opportunity, often resort to violent protest and direct and indirect (digital) harassment of those they identify as fascist, racist, or on the far right (alt right). They also tend to be anti-capitalist, and extremists among them have been investigated by the FBI and the Department of Homeland Security.

AND FASCISM?

Words are conveyers of thoughts, ideas, and emotions. Unless you tie them down to a dictionary definition, they can be used (and misused) in different ways to communicate different things.

The *Merriam-Webster Dictionary* defines *fascism* as

> a political philosophy, movement, or regime (such as that of the Fascisti) that exalts nation and often race above the individual and that stands for a centralized autocratic government headed by a dictatorial leader, severe economic and social regimentation, and forcible suppression of opposition.[1]

For an Antifa activist roaming the streets of Seattle or San Francisco to call conservative speakers visiting local campuses (supposed bastions of free speech) "fascists" seems disingenuous,

---

1 *Merriam-Webster Dictionary*, s.v. "fascism," accessed June 8, 2020, https://www.merriam-webster.com/dictionary/fascism.

as Antifa's own tactics and political philosophies smack more of fascism than do their targets'. Certainly, this is so when baseball bats, helmets, and masks are used to forcibly suppress opposition to leftist views of tolerance and openness. These activists have co-opted and bastardized terminology used commonly in the average American narrative for their own ends of demonizing any opposition to their worldview.

Let us take the matter a step further. Is fascism left, or right?

A favorite smear of those on the left toward anyone on the right is to call such a person a "fascist"—add "pig" if you like. Fascism is claimed to be a phenomenon of the political "righty," whoever he or she might be.

It helps to examine the key philosopher behind the ideology, just as Adam Smith is behind capitalism and Karl Marx is behind Marxism/socialism.

Giovanni Gentile, born in Italy in 1875, was the official "philosopher of fascism" and a loyal supporter of the Italian dictator Benito Mussolini.[2] Gentile served on the Grand Fascist Council of Italy in the 1920s, and as minister of education he remained faithful to fascism till its fall in 1943. He died in 1944.

Simply put, he saw two opposing views of democracy:

---

2   *Encyclopedia of Philosophy*, s.v. "Gentile, Giovanni," updated April 29, 2020, https://www.encyclopedia.com/humanities/encyclopedias-almanacs-transcripts-and-maps/gentile-giovanni-1875-1944.

> liberal democracy, where individualism and personal rights are taken too far and thus become selfish; and

> "true democracy," where individuals willingly subordinate themselves to the state (collective), which of necessity becomes increasingly totalitarian to establish better control to make things work on a large scale.

Gentile saw the public community as a family, where all were in it together. His family analogy is attractive to leftists today who talk of the human family, unity, fairness, and equity. Gentile also saw fascism as a form of socialism, indeed, its most workable form. Whereas socialism mobilizes people according to their economic class (proletariat, etc.), fascism adds a layer of national identity to the mix. Fascists are thus left-wing socialists with a strong national identity. Italian fascism sure displayed these characteristics under Mussolini.

By the way, the word *Nazi* comes from *Nationalsozialist*, German for "National socialist." The Nazis of the 1930s and '40s adopted a lot of socialist measures in the establishment of their fascist/nationalistic state. Adolf Hitler and Mussolini were bedfellows in the run-up to the Second World War.

Mussolini turned Gentile's doctrine into action orchestrating state control and influence in all aspects of society, not just the political sphere.

In truth you cannot escape recognizing the

interconnectedness of everything: economics, education, human relationships, politics, and law. This interconnection is a fact of modern life. The degree of centralized control is key.

Even in America today we see varying degrees of centralized control, whether at the local, the state, or the national level. Consider education, health care, energy, and security as examples of what we may call centralized or state-directed capitalism. Big government by way of more laws, and tax-funded programs are perennially pushed by the Left as a solution to many if not most societal ills. Increased taxation is thus the favorite source of revenue to pay for the never-ending programs legislated into law.

In short, today's Left (and *not* the Right) appears more and more like Gentile's fascism of the first half of the twentieth century. There remains quite a strong national identity in America, but it is increasingly undergirded by a left-leaning socialism and not the more traditional individual capitalistic approach to life's interactions.

3

GLOBALISM DEFINED, AND HOW IT CONNECTS WITH SOCIALISM

A NEW WORLD ORDER?

> *Why do the nations rage,*
>   *and the people plot a vain thing?*
> *The kings of the earth set themselves,*
>   *and the rulers take counsel together,*
>   *against the LORD and against His Anointed, saying,*
> *"Let us break Their bonds in pieces*
>   *and cast away Their cords from us."*
>
> *He who sits in the heavens shall laugh;*
>   *the Lord shall hold them in derision.*
>
> —PSALM 2:1-4

AGENDA

Globalism may be defined as an understanding that all countries are inextricably linked to one another in the modern world. With globalism, both economic and foreign policies of each country should be planned with a view to fostering cooperation and stability at an international level. It involves a largely unfettered flow of people, goods, and information across national borders/boundaries of nation-states. Cultural, technological, social, and economic networks are to be facilitated by overarching organizations such as the United Nations, the European Union, and the World Council of Churches.

Leftists (and some right of center) tend to favor globalism, as it ties in with their agenda for sociopolitical change. A "one-world" government would more readily orchestrate a "New World Order," where global justice, peace, and prosperity would exist. National values and practices would need to submit to the worldwide collective. In this brave new world, the global elite (comprising largely unelected bureaucrats and "experts") are in a real sense unaccountable to the people. It is no longer government of, by and for the people through their elected representatives.[1]

Mass migration, say today's globalists (think Middle East and Europe from the 2010s on), is necessary for

---

1 Abraham Lincoln, in his Gettysburg Address (1863), urged dedication to a government "of the people, by the people, for the people." See *Encyclopedia Britannica*, s.v. "Gettysburg Address," https://www.britannica.com/event/Gettysburg-Address.

GLOBALISM DEFINED...

economic growth. The aging populations in Europe require a fresh input of workers at lower economic levels to bolster their economies.

Globalists favor strong and extensive centralized government, where power is increasingly concentrated in the hands of ever fewer people. These elites can more easily impose their worldview and agenda on the masses.

Donald Trump, and other leaders like him in Brazil and the UK (think the "Brexit" movement to leave the European Union), have pushed back against globalism in some respects. This has precipitated an intense and heated resistance by those who are vested in globalism.

The "America first" Trump doctrine is being called out as reactionary, even racist, fascist, or bigoted. The drive for global citizenship has been slowed somewhat by these populist movements, which have been heralded by some and vilified by others.

Globalists do not favor national sovereignty, nationalism, and/or self-governance. Rather, they push for open borders and free trade, even a one-world currency. In the US they oppose border security (no wall).

In the church world, orthodox and theologically conservative Christians believe that the globalist push for a one-world government amounts to rebellion against God, who alone can unite the world and usher in lasting peace and prosperity. Leftist globalists seek to create a humanistic utopia, where God and His grand purposes for nations is not involved. Christianity is seen as "exclusivist" and opposed to the value of "inclusiveness." In this line of thought, all religions are equally valid and should be open to a one-world religion.

The true, inclusive heart of the God of the Bible is largely misunderstood, if not ignored (think, "for God so loved *the world*," John 3:16, emphasis added). His plan for both individuals and nation groups was outlined by the apostle Paul in the Bible. Preaching to his sophisticated Athenian audience about God's plan for distinct nations, the apostle said:

> He has made from one blood every nation of men to dwell on all the face of the earth, and has determined their *preappointed times and the boundaries* of their dwellings, so that they should seek the Lord, in the hope that they might grope for Him and find Him, though He is not far from *each one* of us. (Acts 17:26–27, emphasis added)

Notice the words "every nation" and "the boundaries of their dwellings." Nations, in all their diversity, are to seek the Lord and discover His purposes both individually and as nations or people groups.

The sovereignty of nations tends toward liberty, not away from it. Centralization tends toward tyranny, especially when you factor in fallen human nature. Only those submitted to the loving lordship of Christ and transformed from selfishness and greed to selfless sacrifice and service are really qualified as public servants.

GLOBALISM DEFINED...

When you observe nature, diversity does not necessarily mean disunity. A variety of plants can and do coexist in the world's ecosystems, especially where humans do not overly interfere. Blind uniformity can and does lead to problems. Monoculture (the growing of one crop on one piece of land) produces problems, whereas a balanced and biodiverse approach to food production is more sustainable and healthier.

Globalism requires that people conform to dictates from experts and elites, who often bypass scrutiny and escape accountability through democratic elections and other checks and balances.

SOCIALISM AND COMMUNISM

Technically, socialism and Communism are not identical, although both are opposed to free market capitalism. Communism tends to be more "left" than socialism and makes fewer concessions to market capitalism and electoral democracy. Democratic socialism is seen by some as a stepping-stone to pure Communism, which produces strong one-party states that ban most forms of political dissent. True democracy has no place in a socialist or Communist state.

Communism had its intellectual and ideological roots in Karl Marx and Friedrich Engels's pamphlet titled *The Communist Manifesto*. It was published in 1848, and it laid out a theory of history where the struggle between economic classes would result in the overthrow of the bourgeoisie class, who controlled the means of production (and thus wealth). In a violent revolution the workers (proletariat) would gain control of the means of production through the centralized government, which, after a while, would fade away, producing in the end a classless society and economy based on common ownership. Political processes would save mankind and usher in utopia, or so they hoped.

Age-old institutions of religion and the family were considered instruments of social control used by the ruling class to subjugate the working class and would therefore have to be abandoned.

In the twentieth century the Bolshevik Revolution of 1917 kicked off the drive for the establishment of a Communist state, which became the Soviet Union (USSR). This union of Soviet socialist republics began to dissolve in 1991.

For Lenin, a key player in the revolution and a founder of twentieth-century Communism in Russia, socialism was a distinct stage between capitalism and communism. The end justified the means in the Bolshevik drive for power. The end game was "pure" Communism, which was never really achieved, as history shows. There were serious problems in making Communism work, one of which was the deaths of tens of millions through political violence and famine under Stalin's leadership in the USSR. Chairman Mao's Cultural Revolution in the People's Republic of China also resulted in millions losing their lives in his push to impose Communism upon the Chinese people.

Class differences between the ruling bourgeoise and working proletariat, rather than being eliminated, were substituted with enormously wealthy Communist Party ruling eco-political cliques, who benefited from their connections to state-owned enterprises, and workers, now largely dependent on state programs and handouts.

Socialism implies the social or communal ownership of the means of production, and Communism insists on the equitable shared consumption of that production through centralized control. Redistribution of wealth by strong government intervention ensures that no one has too little (and indeed no one has too much)—theoretically, at least.

In the United States Communism is still considered bad, but socialism is increasingly celebrated and defended as being good and fair. A generation of neo-socialists has been bred through the school system. Democratic socialism is hawked by the likes of Bernie Sanders, a lifetime supporter of Communism.

Various aspects of socialism were experimented with during the latter half of the nineteenth century and certainly in the twentieth century. Leaders have always tried to arrange a more egalitarian distribution of wealth, better conditions for workers, and common ownership of land and manufacturing equipment. Hard-left brands of socialism have called for a radical societal overhaul, whereas more moderate types opt for more gradual changes in society through policy-change victories. Government regulations concerning workplace safety, minimum wages, pension schemes, social insurance safety nets, and universal "free" health care have been advocated, legislated, and enforced over time. Ever-increasing taxation has been the engine to pay for such endeavors.

After the two world wars, western Europe experienced a surge in socialist political parties. Even the recently decolonized countries of Africa, Asia, and the Middle East came under heavy socialist influence, albeit with local twists "suited" to unique African cultural expressions.

Liberation movements, such as feminism and the civil rights movement, aligned significantly with socialist ideals. There was a convenient overlap. On the other hand, as we have seen, socialist ideas played a role in fostering movements commonly labeled far right but rooted in leftist ideology. European fascists phrased socialist ideas in nationalist terms, most notably Mussolini in Italy.

CAPITALISM AND SOCIALISM

Is it true to say, "Capitalism is based on human greed, while socialism is based on human need"?

Let us begin with an overview.

Capitalism and socialism are the two most significant socioeconomic systems used to understand the way any society's economy works. The scope of government intervention seems to be key where the capitalist model relies on free market dynamics to foster wealth creation and innovation and to regulate corporate behavior. Freedom of choice is encouraged, and the success or failure of any endeavor occurs in an environment of market competition that drives efficiency.

The socialist model of the economy incorporates

elements of centralized government planning that ensures equality of opportunity and even economic outcome.

Most countries display some sort of mix of the two falling somewhere between the two poles.

Capitalism

> *She considers a field and buys it;*
> *from her profits she plants a vineyard.*
>
> —PROVERBS 31:16

In this type of economy, businesses and property are owned and controlled by individuals or corporations, not the government. The law of supply and demand drives the price and production of goods and services. Theoretically, enterprises make the best and cheapest products for consumers to choose from in the market. Owners are motivated to be as efficient as they can in producing, marketing, and selling goods and services. In this way society's needs are met. The profit motive is a central feature of capitalism.

Inspiration produces motivation, and perspiration is the follow-through that causes growth. Put another way, an idea (to meet a need) is created, a business is organized, and a risk is taken (for example, a loan is taken out to fund the endeavor). In simple terms, banks are the agencies that provide capital for business.

Efficiency in the capitalist system takes precedence over equality, as inequality is what drives innovation and pushes economic development.

Socialism

Here, the state owns and controls the major means of production. Some socialist countries have worker cooperatives, whereas others allow individual ownership but with high taxation rates and stringent government controls to ensure funding and policies to further the equitable distribution of wealth and resources. This might be code for taking from the rich to support the poor. The motive is "fairness." The playing field is supposedly leveled out to produce equal opportunity and, indeed, outcome.

The state becomes the primary employer in socialist economies and can control the unemployment rate even if workers are not producing efficiently and in sync with the market demands.

Most countries fall in between socialism and capitalism where both the private-sector system of capitalism is mixed with a strong public sector to overcome disadvantages of both systems. These mixed economies employ tactics to restrict private monopolies and "undue" concentration of economic power. On the other hand, they also try to restrict central government control of the private sector.

CASE STUDY: DENMARK, A MODERN MARVEL OF SOCIALISM, OR . . .

Denmark is touted as an example of socialism's success. Yes, it does have a high level of taxes and high levels of government spending, characteristic of a socialist approach. Yet, in most other aspects, Denmark is a full-on free market capitalist economy. It maintains strong individual property rights, and opening a business involves little bureaucratic red tape. There are also no minimum wage laws. Denmark is rated near the top in world rankings for free market countries by the Heritage Foundation (USA) and the Fraser Institute (Canada).

Citizens of Denmark do enjoy plenty of handouts but can only do so at the expense of high taxes generated from a strong history of free market capitalism. Denmark after World War II created a lot of wealth before it swung strongly toward a welfare state. Early efforts to redistribute wealth in the 1970s led to an economic crisis that has taken decades to sort out.

For example, the Danish equivalent of US Social Security is being replaced by personally responsible 401(k) programs. Supposedly free health care is paid for by high taxes; so too is "free" education. Abuses in this system—such as students staying on perpetually to get continued welfare—amount to welfare dependency, something the Danes are trying to address now.

In short, Denmark is not a modern socialist paradise. Until COVID-19 the average American earner had approximately 27 percent more money to dispose of after taxes than the average Dane.

AGENDA

WHAT ABOUT BRAZIL?
Brazil in the 1990s had one of the most promising economies in the Southern Hemisphere. As the fifth-largest country in the world in area and population, and with its abundant natural resources, it was looking forward to major progress after suffering inflation and political turmoil.

However, when Lula da Silva was elected president in 2003, the country began to lurch toward socialism as he embraced the Workers' Party policies. It was a form of "socialism lite," not quite as stringent as in Venezuela and Cuba, but nevertheless characterized by voluminous new regulations and massive government spending. This included everything from "infrastructure" programs, civil service salary increases, welfare programs, and expanded government worker employment, and even large early retirement pensions were granted.

As power and money became more concentrated in the hands of the expanded political class, the average Brazilian began to realize that the happy talk about doing good for the people (i.e., socialist propaganda) was just that: happy talk. They saw that big government did not necessarily equal good government and that corrupt socialism should be rejected. It was not delivering the goods, as they say.

Jair Bolsonaro, an ex-military officer of the conservative Social Liberty Party, was elected president in January 2019 after running against a committed socialist and even surviving a serious assassination attempt in September 2018. He ran on opposing socialism and combating corruption as a law-and-order candidate, as well as committing to an agenda that promotes small or limited central government. Political appointees who were running state-owned companies and enterprises were to be removed to reduce government intervention in the economy.

Bolsonaro is a conservative, holding pro-life and pro-gun positions while opposing abortion on demand and loose immigration policies. Therefore, he has been labeled by leftists with the usual slew of terms: *racist*, *misogynist*, *homophobic*, and *sexist*.

He has aligned himself more and more with the United States under Donald Trump and even been likened to him in his populist/nationalist appeal. He has pushed back on Chinese globalism or imperialism and seeks to support democracies like those in the United States and Israel.

The future has yet to tell how well Brazil will be able to combat and correct its socialist tendencies in the twenty-first century.

AND VENEZUELA?

Venezuela had a functioning democracy, a rapidly developing economy, and a growing middle class before things were turned upside down once Hugo Chávez gained power in 1998. A new constitution was adopted, and new laws were passed to redistribute land and wealth. Up till then health care, education, and foreign investment rates were trending in a positive direction, but today Venezuela is considered a failed state, where the power and water supply is unreliable, and basic consumer goods, such as toilet paper and bread, are in chronic short supply. Inflation has risen sharply, and crime has skyrocketed. Today, freedom of the press is almost nonexistent, and democratic institutions have largely been replaced by a dictatorship. Opposition leaders who try to represent the true situation there are often jailed, and people stand in lines to get food. On a national scale people have lost an average of nineteen pounds, a situation that is cynically described as the "Maduro diet," after Nicolás Maduro, the current president (Chávez died in 2013).

During Chávez's regime, economically, the country emphasized its oil exports and became quite vulnerable because of this reliance. Now, under Maduro, price controls and a heavily centralized economy add to Venezuela's difficulties as it still pursues socialism.

Incidentally, Hugo Chávez campaigned under the slogan "Hope and Change." He labeled capitalists and their corporations as evil and greedily stealing from the people. Chávez drew inspiration from Cuba's Fidel Castro, a radical Communist, and was even celebrated by some well-known Hollywood celebrities: Sean Penn, Danny Glover, and Harry Belafonte.

However, Chávez's new government soon ran out of OPM—other people's money. People in Venezuela who could get their money out of the country, did.

Today Venezuela is largely isolated, with many international airlines refusing to fly there. The country's socialist policies have clearly failed, and attempts to blame it on reactionary capitalists seem to point toward a harder road back from the current difficulties.

CHINESE COMMUNISM

Much has been written about Chinese Communism in the twentieth century and more recently in the twenty-first century, with its obvious worldwide imperialism. It has become the new "colonialist" power in Africa.

The mind-boggling outcomes of brutal socialist/Communist policies in China in the twentieth century (where upwards of fifty to sixty million people lost their lives before their time) have been replaced by today's more "sophisticated," top-down, centralized control measures. "Social credit scoring" of the populace there involves giving advantages to individuals who behave in accordance with the central government's view of good citizenship. It goes way beyond the financial side of one's creditworthiness (and thus access to loan resources) and now encompasses such elements as one's social media activities, health records (such as vaccinations), online purchases, social circle, tax records, and legal matters. Even data from two hundred million surveillance cameras and facial recognition software is being employed to aggregate social credit scores. The social credit score system, now fully implemented, allows "the trustworthy to roam everywhere under heaven while making it hard for the discredited to take a single step."[2]

---

2   Bradford Betz, "What Is China's Social Credit System?," Fox News, updated May 4, 2020, https://www.foxnews.com/world/what-is-china-social-credit-system.

AGENDA

Since 9/11 the broadening of surveillance of US citizens by various intelligence agencies puts the United States not far behind China in all this. Cameras, drones, vaccination IDs, and smartphone location tracking are already on the table, especially now that the COVID-19 event of 2020 has hit. "Contact tracing" has now been added to the common vernacular.

China's record of human rights violations, notably the Tiananmen Square massacre of 1989 in Beijing, and the Hong Kong street protests of 2019–20, are certainly washed (through censorship) from Chinese mainstream consciousness. Western countries who lean left seem to give China a pass on its human rights violations. Perhaps it is because they import multiple billions of dollars' worth of goods and services from a Chinese economy driven by cheap labor.

The COVID-19 event seems to have had the effect in China of controlling dissent. The Hong Kong street protests and even those protests against extreme pollution in the Wuhan province have been shut down because of the medical lockdown measures implemented there. China is front and center in the World Health Organization (WHO) push for worldwide mandated vaccines and the attendant tracking and surveillance measures. China even stands to benefit from the shock wave to the American economy, as the US adopted draconian measures to fight the worldwide pandemic. China seems to have used the pandemic to control increasingly restless and desperate people under their Communist Party rule.

NAZISM VERSUS COMMUNISM

Both Communists and National Socialists, or Nazis, caused great suffering for millions in the twentieth century. Joseph Stalin, Adolf Hitler, and Mao Zedong (who ruled China from 1949 until his death in 1976) between them presided over an estimated one hundred million deaths through war and "cultural revolution." Some argue that Communism was responsible for more deaths than Nazism, yet because of widespread ignorance of the Communist record, it gets off with lighter condemnation. How so?

Leftists have never loathed Communism, and it is not depicted in colleges and universities as something that is evil. In fact, the leftists lean toward Communism as a viable alternative to Western capitalism–based democracy.

The systematic genocidal slaughter of approximately six million Jews in the Holocaust during the Second World War under Hitler and the Nazis is well documented, whereas the Communist slaughter under first Stalin and then Mao is not so well documented. The official Chinese narrative has largely denied the horrors of Mao's holocaust among his own people. In contrast the Germans have largely owned up to the reality of multiple millions losing their lives in the name of National Socialism.

Sadly, Stalin and Mao are still officially revered in their countries.

Oddly, world opinion frowns less upon the killing by Communists of their own people compared to the killing of mostly other peoples by German Nazis. Then too, the world describes the Second World War as the last "good" war because it was fought against the evils of German Nazism and Japanese fascism.[3] Other, later wars against Communist regimes (the Korean conflict and the Vietnam War) were not "good" wars.

TIE-IN WITH GLOBALISM

The kingdoms of this world have become the kingdoms of our Lord and of His Christ, and He shall reign forever and ever!

—REVELATION 11:15

We started this chapter looking at globalism as an overarching worldview that sees a need for international cooperation and control. Certainly, Hitler and his Nazi cronies wanted to establish a one-thousand-year Reich (or realm where the "pure" race would rule). Empire building is not foreign to all peoples and times. There was the Roman Empire, the Spanish Empire (Hispanic Monarchy), and the British Empire, to name a few.

The Bible contrasts the "kingdoms of this world" with the "kingdom of God." Who is it that ultimately rules a man's heart? Surely it cannot be some fallen and often corrupt politician in a remote chamber somewhere deciding your fate. Politicians do not always know better how you

---

3   See Bruce Nelan, "1939–1948 War: The Last Good War," *Time*, March 9, 1998.

GLOBALISM DEFINED...

should live. The kingdom of God is advancing despite man's attempt to factor out God's rule in globalism's misguided machinations. The rampant socialist agenda of the United Nations feeds into worldwide control of globalism. We are told that "global problems need global solutions,"[4] so we should just hand over our individual nation-state liberties to the UN, and they will provide the security that comes from their "experts."

The thing is, the experts have clay feet too.

---

[4] UN News Centre, "Global Problems Need Global Solutions, UN Officials Tell Ministers at Development Forum," United Nations Department of Economic and Social Affairs, July 17, 2017, https://www.un.org/development/desa/en/news/intergovernmental-coordination/high-level-segment.html.

4

SOCIALISM IN THE UNITED STATES

SERIOUSLY?

Blessed is the nation whose God is the LORD,
The people He has chosen as His own inheritance.

—PSALM 33:12

"One nation under God"... or under government? Think about it. Who is really in charge?

Good old Uncle Sam deserves a separate chapter because this huge example of Western capitalism has not been exempted from creeping socialistic tendencies, especially in the twentieth century and now quite dramatically in the twenty-first century.

AGENDA

It's helpful to take a quick excursion to way back in early western settlement of North America's Eastern Seaboard in the 1600s. The early European settlers sought escape from religious persecution and experimented with socialism in the new community they established in Plymouth, Massachusetts. The experiment failed, and over time the current, free market capitalist system developed.

At first, the early Pilgrims decided they would practice collectivism, a form of socialism where all labor was communal, both in food production and in domestic household labor. Incentive for personal gain was lost, and the project failed miserably after a short while. Even the pious and decent Puritans committed to survival together could not make the communal approach work. They soon learned a valuable lesson about human nature and community.

Each family was later given their own lot of land to grow their own food, which they did, and produced so much surplus beyond their own needs that they were then able to trade with local Indians. The fledgling colony soon prospered, and these colonists' commitment to pursue religious freedom and private ownership paved the way for a later establishment of the American Republic and its Constitution.

Much later, America began incorporating a measure of socialism into the nation's underlying government structure and economy when Franklin Delano Roosevelt (FDR) instituted the "New Deal" in response to the crisis of the Great Depression. This deal incorporated a series of programs, public work projects, financial reforms, and regulations enacted between 1933 and 1939.

The National Recovery Administration was formed in 1933, launching a top-down, centralized, bureaucratic quagmire of collectivism where virtually all industry, manufacturing, and retail business was corralled into cartels. These entities had the power to set prices and wages and even levels of production, things more akin to socialism than to capitalism, with its free market forces of supply and demand. A special enforcement agency even operated to ensure that the myriads of regulations were being enforced.

Many urban youths were sent off to forested land to be part of the Civilian Conservations Corps (CCC). Along with the Works Progress Administration (WPA) and the Social Security Administration (SSA), efforts were made to impose central government regulations on banking practices. Large infrastructure projects were initiated: roads, bridges, dams, and so on, where large numbers of workers were employed by the government. The Tennessee Valley Authority (TVA) was a clear example of the government trying to spur development through infrastructure projects.

Interestingly, the effects of the Bolshevik-led Russian Revolution of 1917 were felt in America through efforts by the labor unions of the day pushing for a brand of socialism. However, by the 1930s leaders from the Social Democratic Party of America (with its roots in Karl Marx's writings), and the Communist Party of the United States were not making significant inroads into the political scene.

AGENDA

So, the labor unions pledged their loyalty to FDR (Franklin Delano Roosevelt) and the New Deal, becoming registered Democrats. The National Industrial Recovery Act of 1933 (NIRA) formed the heart of FDR's New Deal, which the unions would easily support. In fact, some argue that FDR's plan was modeled after Stalin's five-year plans employed in Communist Russia.

Then in 1933 FDR pressured Congress to pass the Agricultural Adjustment Act, which gave the federal government wide-ranging control over the nation's farms. The president ordered the destruction of crops and the slaughter of millions of pigs to control falling food prices. At the time FDR talked of a "controlled economy, common sense, and social decency"; all the while his policies only served to erode states' rights and consolidate control at the federal level. The nation was leaning toward socialism.[1]

In the end, the New Deal did not lift America out of the Great Depression. The Second World War did.

The Democratic Party dominated the political landscape from 1933 to 1969. During this time Lyndon Baines Johnson further promoted aspects of socialism through his "Great Society" (1964–65), the main goals of which were to eliminate poverty and racial injustice. Major spending

---

1 See Peter Kuznick, Matt Graham, and Oliver Stone, "The Untold History—The Series—Episode B 1920–40. Roosevelt, Hitler, Stalin: The Battle of Ideas," *Indispensable Nation*, https://theindispensablenation.com/episode-b-1920---40-roosevelt-hitler-stalin-the-battle-of-ideas.html.

programs were initiated to address concerns about education, medical care, urban problems, and rural poverty. Today, the "War on Poverty" still goes on, even after billions and billions have been spent on programs to address "structural and systemic" problems in society. Unfortunately, the perennial problem of the human heart cannot be addressed from the outside in. Change comes from the inside out. Reform always follows repentance.

THEN THERE WAS 9/11

What have the 9/11 event in 2001 and the PATRIOT Act have to do with socialism?

The shockwave of 9/11 produced a legislative reaction just forty-five days after the disaster. The controversial PATRIOT Act (later renewed as the USA Freedom Act) focused on fighting terrorism and enjoyed support from large majorities of both the House of Representatives and the Senate. The PATRIOT Act of 2001 was written *before* the 9/11 attacks and quickly passed into law riding on a wave of fear not unlike that surrounding the coronavirus event of 2020. Civil liberties advocates who expressed concern about government overreach at the time were called unpatriotic as they lamented the loss of "liberty for greater security."

The "war on terror" has become center stage in the national psyche since 9/11, just as the war on the virus has in 2020.

Besides executing the war around the world with newly weaponized technology, strict countermeasures have been included, such as unlimited detention of suspected (not proven) terrorists, without even a hearing. Such detainees, however, do have the right to appeal to the Supreme Court and to sue the authorities, yet the "war" footing is a platform for the suspension of the regular rule of law. The State Department has the right to designate organizations as terrorists without court or congressional review. Secret searches without the suspect's knowledge are also allowed and are not limited to terrorist investigations. Since 9/11 and the enactment of the PATRIOT Act powers, terrorist attacks have continued. Sadly, since Congress first passed the PATRIOT Act some two decades ago, mass surveillance, warrantless wiretapping, and bulk data collection have not stopped a single terrorist attack. We are told that some attacks have been thwarted, yes, but at what expense? History is yet to decide.

Civil liberty protections being considered at this time do little to shield innocent citizens from being caught up in investigations of suspected terrorists. For example, someone may snitch on you for engaging in suspect activity, like buying fertilizer (used by some in bomb making), and you can be investigated without knowing it is happening.

Some argue that the PATRIOT Act shifted the US toward a more top-down authoritarian form of government that looks more and more like the socialist totalitarian regimes of Russia and China than a nation committed to individual liberty and limited government guaranteed by the Constitution.

The coronavirus event of late 2019 and early 2020 may

even have the effect of pushing back against passing "sunset" clauses of the USA Freedom Act that would supposedly have restored a number of the civil liberties eroded in the wake of the 9/11 terrorist attacks, especially the surveillance aspects.

VERY RECENT TRENDS IN THE USA

The economic meltdown of 2020 due to the COVID-19 lockdowns seemingly points toward an orchestrated weakening of the revitalized middle class that Trump was trying to strengthen with his policies. The other side of the equation is the entrenchment of an upper-class, wealthy, minority "elite"—the educated experts who know better: brave new technocratic masters of the New World Order. The third group—the permanent underclass of poor people struggling to survive economically—serve, in this scenario, as useful drones or worker bees. This smacks of the classic "class struggle" dynamics of socialism.

Too much to swallow? The stuff of conspiracy? It is not impossible, taking the twentieth-century history of socialism into account. The drama is unfolding as of this writing.

The federal government–motivated financial "recovery" programs (like the Small Business Administration loans) introduced in April 2020 are an attempt to support the middle class and restart the US economy. In a modern mixed economy, these measures, although looking like twenty-first-century socialism, may well be the right thing to do. History will tell.

On to the "Green New Deal." This folly is espoused

by the extreme leftist wing of the Democratic Party and promulgated by AOC—Representative Alexandria Ocasio-Cortez. It amounts to socialism mixed in with the environmentalist agenda in a stew that smells good to some but to others is downright fishy.

As the saying goes, green is the new red.[2]

The goal of environmentalism is not just about climate change and saving the planet, but is a push to overhaul the entire US economy. That is the agenda behind the agenda. The economy would supposedly transition away from fossil fuels within ten years while simultaneously providing federal jobs and health care for all. It would advance social, economic, racial, regional, and even gender-based justice and equality through cooperative and public ownership.

Classical socialism once again, all in the name of laudable causes, like protecting and indeed "saving" the planet, and "justice" that no reasonable person should oppose, right? To do so would make you bigoted, a "denier" and a fringe reactionary. The $93 trillion cost would not be a problem—just spread it over ten years; hopefully you would not have run out of other people's money by then.

---

2   See Stephen Moore, "Green Is the New Red," Heritage Foundation, February 13, 2019, https://www.heritage.org/energy-economics/commentary/green-the-new-red.

TRUMP, POPULISM, AND "AMERICA FIRST" NATIONALISM

Donald J. Trump rode down an escalator in Trump Tower on June 16, 2015, and precipitated a wave of populist political excitement that swept him into the White House in November 2016 in an upset victory over the Establishment favorite, Hillary Clinton.

Tired of the same old same old political theater every four years, the American public noticed something was going on, went to his never-seen-before rallies, and voted him in at the booths, to the utter dismay of many.

Trump ruffled feathers everywhere: political establishment on both sides of the aisle, media pundits, voters, bankers, Hollywood celebrities, you name it. Something was happening, and it was, Trump himself would put it, "huge."

He got to work putting "America First" through a series of executive orders, policy changes, and political pressure that impacted the economy, the military, in what was a game-changing set of fulfilled campaign promises that caught the attention of many onlookers.

Despite severe coordinated efforts to reverse the election result (accusations of Russian collusion and impeachment proceedings), Trump survived and even came out on top with approval ratings on the up. It looked as though all that Trump had done in his first three years as president augured well for a conservative-based future. Growth of central government had been somewhat curtailed—deregulation had begun; better trade deals with Mexico, Canada, and China had been secured. Companies were being encouraged to bring jobs back to American soil, and the president even took a harder line with North Korea, Russia, and Iran on the international front.

Trump threw a spanner in the works to globalists all over. His appearances at the UN, G7, and G20 meetings, in Davos, Switzerland, were often met with consternation as he pushed back on the globalist agenda. He even went so far as to say that socialism in the United States would never be, as he tweeted away, trolling everyone from the "Never Trumpers" in his own party to the radical wing of the Democratic Party, AOC, and the squad of leftist newcomers to Congress.

He was attacked relentlessly from all sides, while supporters of his agenda shook their heads at the obvious media bias and downright dishonesty. He was accused of fostering an unhealthy return to autocratic white male–dominated nationalism by some, while others portrayed his actions and policies as a return to good old American patriotism. The deep state swamp was being drained, and the creatures were reacting.

And then COVID-19 hit.

5

WHAT DID GEORGE ORWELL SAY ABOUT FACEBOOK AND YOUTUBE?

NOTHING?

> *"And you shall know the truth, and the truth shall make you free."*
>
> —JOHN 8:32

Of course, George Orwell said nothing directly about Facebook and YouTube in his works, but he was remarkably prophetic when it comes to our world in the twenty-first century.

Orwell published the novel *1984* in June 1949. It dealt with the themes of government overreach, mass surveillance, and repressive regimentation by totalitarian authorities.

AGENDA

These amounted to severe curtailment of individual freedoms, and propaganda and official deception played a big role.

The novel is set in a world of super states after a global war. The fictional nation of Oceania is controlled by a party leader called "Big Brother," whose henchmen can surveil all activity inside your home and out by means of two-way "telescreens." Wow.

Oceania is divided into three classes:

- the upper-class Inner Party—the elite ruling minority—representing 2 percent of the population

- the professional-managerial–class Outer Party—the middle class—representing 13 percent of the population.

- the lower-class Proletariat—the working class—representing 85 percent of the population

The government, or Party, controls the people through four ministries:

- the Ministry of Peace, which deals with war and defense

- the Ministry of Plenty, which deals with economic affairs (starvation and rationing)

- the Ministry of Love, which deals with law and order (torture and brainwashing)

- the Ministry of Truth, which deals with news, entertainment, education, and art (propaganda)

(Perhaps George Orwell would have used the term *fake news* if he were to observe what is going on today.)

In Orwell's novel, the "Thought Police" ensured conformity to the party line, and a new language, called "Newspeak," was developed to corral the masses into a reduced form of thinking and communication. The key word in Newspeak is *blackwhite*, a word with two mutually contradictory meanings. When applied to an opponent, it contradicts the plain facts. It is whatever you want it to mean to suit your purpose. This system of thought is known as "doublethink." You may recognize some of this going on in our modern culture when it comes to gender matters, and certainly in politics and ethics. When someone is a bigoted fascist and he calls you one . . . you get the picture: classical psychological projection.

Censorship and surveillance are two aspects in Orwell's novel worth considering when it comes to our world today. Orwell also wrote the book *Animal Farm* in 1945 wherein he satirized the Russian Revolution and rise of Stalin into a repressive dictator. The saying "some animals are more equal than others" is famous for its criticism of the whole socialist/Communist endeavor to create a society where people can be free, equal, and happy.

AGENDA

The hugely popular and influential platforms, such as YouTube, Twitter, Facebook, and the Google search engine, have defined our modern lives and have most notably come to light recently as agents of sociopolitical change. The controllers of these enterprises have been accused of sophisticated forms of censorship through their algorithms, shadow banning, and removal of posts with which they disagree according to guidelines that supposedly protect viewers. Shadow banning occurs when a user or his or her content is blocked partially or completely from an online community in such a way that the user will not readily know it has happened.

It has become commonplace for mostly conservative accounts to be affected in this way. Commentators have said that Facebook has the capability to target an audience in such a way as to sway their opinions and actions. This includes posts that target specific demographics before an election. This has become a concern for upcoming presidential elections especially.

Free speech norms have also been eroded through the newly defined "hate speech" objections. So-called hate speech posts can be and are banned regularly. The top areas where individuals or groups are attacked are race, religion, ethnic origin, sexual orientation, disability, and gender. On the surface most of this is acceptable, but increasingly a leftist and postmodern bias is driving this sort of censorship. A "new morality" is being established that runs counter to the Judeo-Christian worldview that most seemingly still adhere to, at least in the US. It may even be accurate to say that the worldview of most of the controllers of these modern information and communication platforms (YouTube, Facebook, Twitter, Google) tend toward leftist socialism and globalism.

In March 2020, during the coronavirus pandemic saga, YouTube let its viewers know that it would resort more than normal to AI (artificial intelligence) to moderate and take down videos that violate policy, as many of its human reviewers had been sent home to limit the spread of the virus. YouTube admitted that many videos may be taken down that did not actually violate policy.

The message seemed to be, "Sorry. Our censorship is not perfect at this stage."

By the way, PragerU, an internet "university" led by Denis Prager, uses YouTube extensively to promote its conservative agenda via short videos of a political, philosophical, environmental, and economic nature. A significant number of PragerU's YouTube posts have been taken down by YouTube as violating user policies. Prager has been forced to take the matter to court, as he argues that his and his contributors' material is unfairly being censored. YouTube argues that it is not acting as a publisher, only as a responsible "platform." YouTube wants it both ways: when it suits them in protecting their leftist agenda, they act as a publisher exercising the right to drop content, while acting like a platform in other situations, where content is deemed suitable.

Facebook, with founder Mark Zuckerberg at the helm,

adopts community standards to process and sometimes delete or censor posts deemed racist or sexist, hate speech, anything deemed to be terrorist in nature, and so on. Where things get trickier is in its privacy practices.

The privacy matter came to a head when Facebook's entanglement with Cambridge Analytica, a political consultancy firm that improperly accessed eighty-seven million Facebook users' names, likes, and other personal information for political advertising, became public. Zuckerberg was questioned by a special congressional hearing in Washington, DC.

It is said that other malicious actors have scraped information from Facebook's two billion users. Facebook has also been accused of censoring conservative content, and even developing the computing ability to specifically target sensitive voters in an election and steer them toward a desired result.

Zuckerberg, a thirty-five-year-old billionaire, back in December 2015 pledged to transfer nearly all his Facebook stock to an LLC (rather than a foundation) controlled by him and wife Priscilla. This wealth is intended to address health and public education concerns by connecting the global community with an information infrastructure that facilitates problem-solving of issues such as poverty, civil and national strife, climate change challenges, and pandemic prevention. Such issues can best be addressed in concert with others globally. Zuckerberg describes himself as a capitalist, yet proposes universal basic income (UBI), a feature of modern socialism.

In April 2020, when people in the US began to tire of state

governor overreach in implementing lockdown guidelines to prevent the spread of coronavirus and to "flatten the curve," Facebook took down posts that promoted and organized protests. Zuckerberg, in an interview with CNN's George Stephanopoulos, called such posts "harmful misinformation."[1] This must point toward totalitarianism at its "capitalist" worst! After all, the First Amendment has been shredded in the name of medical mitigation against COVID-19.

How about this: unmanned drones were used to monitor (spy on) citizens in Elizabeth, New Jersey, an action the mayor lauded as saving lives. The drones were made in China, which has used such technology to spy on its own citizens. The Chinese-affiliated company DJI also donated the drones to twenty-two states to help them in their fight against "unruly protesters." Maybe useful data is being sent back to China? Just asking. Apparently, the Pentagon has banned their use. In New York City Mayor DeBlasio ordered eight million citizens to report (spy and snitch on) any neighbors and coworkers they felt were noncompliant with lockdown measures in the city.

Sadly, Facebook and YouTube have been marching in lockstep with an ideologically driven mainstream media, not in pursuit of speaking truth to power, but rather speaking to

---

1   Jack Davis, "Zuckerberg: Organizing Anti-Lockdown Protests on Facebook Is 'Harmful Misinformation and We Take That Down,'" *Western Journal*, April 20, 2020, https://www.westernjournal.com/zuckerberg-organizing-anti-lockdown-protests-facebook-harmful-misinformation-take/.

empower increasingly powerful political elites who largely lean left and might well be called socialist if you go back, say, twenty, thirty, or forty, years in America.

New York Governor Cuomo spoke on TV in April 2020 of "reimagining" New York with better public transportation, housing, public safety, health systems, social equality, and use of technology. Seemingly, this is code for left-leaning socialist programs that some authorities want to expand or promote in a push to take advantage of the COVID-19 crisis. After all, one should never let a crisis go to waste," says Rahm Emanuel.[2]

Cuomo went on to say in front of the cameras at his daily briefing in mid-April, "Plan change that we could normally never do unless you had this situation."[3] During March 2020, while lawmakers thrashed out the $2 trillion stimulus bill, leftists tried to slip in aspects not related to the COVID-19 pandemic, like new collective bargaining powers for unions, higher fuel emissions standards for airlines, and expanded wind and solar tax credits. Chuck Schumer's agenda appeared more to be advancing the

---

2   Emma Colton, "Rahm Emanuel Reprises 'Never Let a Crisis Go to Waste' Catchphrase amid Coronavirus Pandemic," *Washington Examiner*, March 24, 2020, https://www.washingtonexaminer.com/news/rahm-emanuel-reprises-never-let-a-crisis-go-to-waste-catchphrase-amid-coronavirus-pandemic.

3   Joshua Caplan, "Gov. Andrew Cuomo Announces Task Force to 'Reimagine' New York," Breitbart, April 20, 2020, https://www.breitbart.com/politics/2020/04/20/gov-andrew-cuomo-announces-task-force-to-reimagine-new-york/.

policies of the Democratic Party than trying to help the economy get back after taking a serious hit due to the draconian lockdown strategies.

6

THE RISE OF SOCIALISM AMONG MILLENNIALS

IS THE SOCIAL JUSTICE EMPHASIS LEGITIMATE?

Your kingdom is an everlasting kingdom,
And Your dominion endures throughout all generations.

—PSALM 145:13

"Millennials" are the generation born between 1981 and 1996 and considered to be the children of my generation, the baby boomers, born between 1946 and 1964.

As far as I can see, every generation has been concerned about injustice. I even remember protesting at university about the injustices of apartheid in South Africa, where I was born and raised. Injustice was central to our student collective consciousness. We were concerned, and still are, about man's inhumanity to man.

Yet, in my case, over time, I became increasingly Christ conscious, as opposed to being cause conscious. Causes without Christ have their limitations, because only He can get down to matters of the human heart with lasting transformation that translates into significant change.

It appears as if millennials easily support causes such as fighting to end sex trafficking, gender discrimination, and voter suppression, as well as efforts to provide clean water, sustainable alternative energies, and so on. Not that any of these are not important. Of course they are. That is not the point, however. The point is that years of socialist-tinged brainwashing at school and at college has slanted their understanding. Of course, there are going to be exceptions, so hold your rocks.

Millennials have been taught that every problem is "systemic" or "structural," like racism, for example. The "system" needs to be changed through protest, activism, and legislation, yet the human heart is largely ignored. The modern solution is to pass legislation that rights the wrongs, allocate more public resources (your taxes) to programs, and set up administrations to help solve the problem. I am sure some of this is true to an extent, but if greed, corruption, and mismanagement (poor stewardship) are not addressed at the individual human heart level, then frustrating flaws are part of the package.

Thankfully, there have been initiatives that deliver

solutions directly to the problems at hand. Most notably, "clean water" groups have done a great job worldwide in digging wells for the disadvantaged. There is much yet to do in providing help in these key areas of basic life needs.

Each generation produces a valuable crop of brilliant entrepreneurs, inventors, and humanitarians. Millennials are no exception. Yet from my perspective it is sad to hear people such as Mark Zuckerberg advancing censorship practices on Facebook that undermine the First Amendment. Zuckerberg is seen as a concerned and neutral humanitarian wanting only to suppress "harmful misinformation" on his platform during the COVID-19 event of 2020. Of course, he and his team are the ones to decide what is "harmful," not you and me.

Bernie Sanders, a longtime socialist (some say Communist), appealed to a younger voting bloc in both the 2016 and the 2020 presidential campaigns for the Democratic Party. How? He sold socialism to millennials as a reasonable, good, moral, common, and ethical approach to solving America's ills and injustices. Sanders has taken advantage of the general ignorance of history, or at least a history that has filtered out socialism's bad track record in countries such as the Soviet Union, China, Venezuela, and Cuba.

Youthful idealism has been exploited by his campaigns. Who would not want their student tuition debt to be forgiven? But idealism must be married to wisdom, which usually is accumulated in time through experience. As a career politician steeped in Western socialism, Sanders has maintained much the same agenda over the years: single-payer health care for all, wealth redistribution, minimum wage increase, a hefty estate tax, expansion of Social Security, free college, and curtailment of free speech or political dissent. His followers are proud to support him because of his "authenticity and integrity."[1]

Both baby boomers and millennials have something to bring to the table in solving society's ills. The generation gap can only be closed through open dialogue and mutual respect.

SOCIAL JUSTICE AND SOCIALISM

He is the Rock, His work is perfect;
   For all His ways are justice,
   A God of truth and without injustice;
   Righteous and upright is He.

—DEUTERONOMY 32:4

"Is this not the fast that I have chosen:
   To loose the bonds of wickedness,
   To undo the heavy burdens,
   To let the oppressed go free,
   And that you break every yoke?

---

[1] See Lauren McCauley, "Hailing 'Authenticity and Integrity,' Cornel West Backs Bernie Sanders," Common Dreams, August 25, 2015, https://www.commondreams.org/news/2015/08/25/hailing-his-authenticity-and-integrity-dr-cornel-west-backs-bernie-sanders.

THE RISE OF SOCIALISM AMONG MILLENNIALS

Is it not to share your bread with the hungry,
And that you bring to your house the poor
who are cast out;
When you see the naked, that you cover him,
And not hide yourself from your own flesh?"

—ISAIAH 58:6-7

Justice is central to God's ways and springs from His heart of compassion and concern for the poor. The Author of all life went to the ultimate lengths to provide for the pinnacle of His creation when He sent His son to the cross to break the back of sin, sickness, and, yes, poverty. Now God expects His people to mirror and model His heart for all men in need.

This pure version of social justice being encouraged in the Bible is in stark contrast to the perversions we find in our modern world. Today, we see socialism and the cries for social justice walking hand in hand. To be fair, there are those who genuinely want to help the poor and needy, but they are going about their cause mostly without God's help. It could be argued that true social justice has been hijacked by secular humanists to further their socialist agendas.

The social justice movement arose in the early nineteenth century during the Industrial Revolution in Europe and aimed to create more egalitarian societies. The capitalistic exploitation of labor and huge wealth and wage gaps that developed prompted early social justice advocates to focus on property, redistribution of wealth, and control of capital. Later, social justice calls expanded to include other aspects of communal life: race relations, the environment, gender, and other manifestations of real and perceived inequality. The focus has been on groups rather than on individual justice and responsibility. In the USA today, white conservative males are blamed for quite a few things just because of their group identity and so-called privileges—never mind any individual's choices or actions within that group. This group-identity politics may be convenient, but to call someone out largely because of his birth race can only be described as racist.

Social justice today often revolves around favoring the oppressed and/or punishing the oppressors, based largely on value judgments made from some sort of moral high ground that these purveyors of identity politics supposedly hold. Nowadays it has become popular to argue that past offenses and injustice reaching way back, even centuries old, need to be addressed through "reparations." The big question is, How far back do you go or, indeed, can you go?

Social justice warriors, or SJWs (often spoken of by the Right in a derogatory manner), tend to adopt causes to fight for gender equality, sexual orientation, rights to health care, and wage equity for the underprivileged, to name a few.

It is my conviction that when someone submits to the lordship of Jesus and follows God's plan for his or her life, that individual will love his or her fellow human beings in such a way as to not enslave them in any way, but to instead serve them from a heart moved with compassion.

Historically, social justice proponents have sought to achieve their goals through both peaceful and non-peaceful means that include government programs (like redistribution of wealth through land appropriation in Zimbabwe, Africa, for example), policies, activism, and sadly, even violent revolution and terrorism. Think ecoterrorists who want to conserve trees and animals yet resort to violently infringing on the rights of their fellow man.

In capitalistic societies, such as the United States, government funding is allocated to support many social justice efforts—like Planned Parenthood, for example. This is the consequence of public rallies, marches, boycotts, lobbying, censorship of certain opposition groups, even direct threats, political thuggery, and violence. The Democratic Party in the US has sadly become a home for the self-identified progressives and socialists.

To be fair, the civil rights movement beginning in the 1950s and continuing into the 1960s, led by Martin Luther King Jr., did usher in radical changes that advanced the interests of African Americans. Discrimination based on race was dealt a severe blow by this movement, the Civil Rights Act of July 2, 1964, being the centerpiece legislation at a national level.

A socially just world does indeed involve ensuring basic human rights and economic egalitarianism. The question is, How do you achieve these goals? Yes, we should work toward equality of *opportunity*, but to force equality of *outcome*, using progressive taxation and income and property redistribution, is inherently flawed. "Taking from the rich to give to the poor" has never worked for long. In the end both are losers.

Of course, the Founding Fathers enshrined key inalienable rights of citizens in the Declaration of Independence and Constitution of the United States way back in the eighteenth century. It cannot be argued that since the nation's inception, all the rich have become wealthy by exploiting the poor. Nevertheless, most socialist literature of the last 150 years has promoted this premise, which may have been true in Karl Marx's time, during the writing of *The Communist Manifesto* (1848), but is not true today.

The dependency culture that very often results when government handout programs run rampant is proving to undermine innovation and motivation among so many recipients of taxpayer-funded welfare payments. Socialism and Communism where tried on a national scale have failed to remove class distinction and wealth inequality. Instead of a nobility/working man distinction, we see a political class/working man distinction arise. Elitism, greed, and exploitation are sadly alive and well in socialist societies, where workers are still exploited by those who hold the levers of power and the middle class is eliminated.

Jesus modeled God's love of and care for the poor. He first brought the message of true freedom (the gospel) to the poor, and then He also fed them. Heart and hand worked together to meet people's needs both temporal and eternal. He also taught His followers to love their neighbor as they loved themselves.

When you read into all teaching in the Bible on wealth and poverty, you find that wealth in itself is not evil; it is only the love of money that the Bible accuses of being "a root of all kinds of evil" (1 Timothy 6:10). Charity and giving to the poor are always voluntary in Scripture, empowered by grace, and not enforced by human government who decides who gets what, when, and where.

The human-centered approach of social justice stands in direct contrast to the God-centered approach. In God's economy, Christ, not the government, is the Savior. To be sure, this side of an eternity to come, there are definite areas of improvement that can be made in helping the needy, but certainly not through largely failed socialist policies, programs, and political action devoid of God's wisdom and perspective.

THE "NEW TOLERANCE"—
OR *INTOLERANT* TOLERANCE

"Judge not, that you be not judged."

—MATTHEW 7:1

Tolerance is a virtue. Yet when it is hijacked, it becomes a tool, even a weapon, to shut down civilized discussion, debate, and development. The "new tolerance" assumes some sort of moral high ground: "I'm right and you are wrong, so I will do all I can to shut you up and/or force your conformity to my views."

True "tolerance," as defined by the *Merriam-Webster Dictionary*, is, among other things:

> "sympathy . . . for beliefs or practices differing from or conflicting with one's own";

"the act of allowing something"; and

"the allowable deviation from a standard"[2]

True tolerance requires disagreement; it cannot exist without it. When you shut down disagreement and demand that everyone accept and agree with your point of view, you do not have tolerance; you have control. Control is something top-down socio-engineers (aka socialists) like to use in advancing their agenda. After all, they believe that they are right, that history is on their side, and that the end justifies the means.

Those leftists or "politically correct" advocates who call those who disagree sexist, bigoted, racist, Islamophobic, homophobic or simply narrow-minded haters are totally counterproductive in establishing and maintaining civilized dialogue with those with whom they disagree.

Religion, politics, and more recently, gender and sexual issues are the stuff of societal relationships that cannot be avoided. In the last couple of years, even those who dared to step outside the strict bounds of the "new tolerant" have been vilified. For example, former world champion tennis player Martina Navratilova, an outspoken lesbian, got herself into trouble when she commented on the unfairness of male transgender athletes competing with those who are

---

2 Merriam-Webster.com, s.v. "tolerance," accessed June 9, 2020, https://www.merriam-webster.com/dictionary/tolerance.

women by birth. She was labeled a bigot.[3] J. K. Rowling of *Harry Potter* fame likewise got into hot water for stating the obvious about male and female differences. She is very left of center, yet when she stepped out of line, she got stepped *on* by the tolerant intolerant.[4]

In the end, who will be the ultimate judge in all this, deciding what is right and moral and fair? In a Judeo-Christian worldview, God is the final supreme court justice. In a self-centered humanistic worldview, we humans are the ultimate judge. In a world where God is excluded, usually the most forceful among us get our way, at least for a time. The end justifies any means to get there. If my cause is "just," then I can use any means to advance it, including lies and misinformation.

When values of truth, integrity, and proper judgment fall in the streets, then you have a major problem. You must not allow true justice to be overrun in your society.

Justice is turned back, and righteousness stands afar off;
For truth is fallen in the street, and equity cannot enter.

—ISAIAH 59:14

---

3 See James Kirkup, "By Branding Martina Navratilova a Bigot, the Trans Lobby Shows How Intolerant and Extreme It Has Become," *Telegraph* (UK), February 21, 2019, https://www.telegraph.co.uk/sport/2019/02/21/martina-navratilova-serving-sense-gender/.

4 See Paul Bois, "J.K Rowling Defends Biological Sex Again, Gets Hate Again," *Daily Wire*, June 6, 2020, https://www.dailywire.com/news/j-k-rowling-defends-biological-sex-again-gets-hate-again.

7

CHURCH AND STATE SEPARATION/SECULAR HUMANISM/SOCIALISM

FREEDOM OF RELIGION OR FREEDOM FROM RELIGION?

> *"I call heaven and earth as witnesses today against you, that I have set before you life and death, blessing and cursing; therefore choose life, that both you and your descendants may live."*
>
> —DEUTERONOMY 30:19

Religion is central to the human experience in all societies. When religious expression is controlled by the authorities, there are problems. In the United States, the Founding Fathers were keenly aware of the downside of this situation and included religious freedom as a fundamental right in what is known as the Bill of Rights in the US Constitution.

The original ten amendments were ratified in December

AGENDA

1791. The First Amendment prohibits government from establishing a state/national religion, as England had done with the state Church of England. The First Amendment also allows for the free practice of religion. In addition, it protected freedom of speech, assembly, and petition.

Here is the text of the First Amendment of the US Constitution:

> Congress shall make no law respecting an establishment of religion, or prohibiting the free exercise thereof; or abridging the freedom of speech, or of the press; or the right of the people peaceably to assemble, and to petition the Government for a redress of grievances.

This and the other amendments have served significantly as hallmarks of modern limited democratic government. Regarding the religion clauses, it is vital to see that the Constitution emphasizes both freedom *of* religion and freedom *from* religion as imposed by government.

When believers look at the matter, they tend to emphasize the first focus: freedom *of* religion. On the other hand, those who are more into man governing himself and finding secular solutions to life's issues and struggles (nonbelievers) tend to emphasize freedom *from* religion. These people point to the phrase "separation between Church & State," which Thomas Jefferson used when he wrote about his views on the two sides of the amendment (establishment and free exercise of religion clauses) to the Danbury Baptists, which he published in a Massachusetts newspaper in January 1802.[1]

This "wall of separation" between church and state has come to be commonly used or abused depending on where a person stands on the church's role in society, especially in matters of state and government. The precise boundaries have been challenged in the courts by both sides, and today many in the church argue that their freedoms have increasingly been eroded by creeping secularization of American society and culture in the twentieth century and now in the twenty-first century.

The lockdown measures adopted by most states following the first American coronavirus diagnoses, which involved shutting down in-person church gatherings, is seen by many as seriously challenging the basic rights of US citizens. Those who argue for continued COVID-19 mitigation measures to continue for months and in some cases years, do so in the face of the First Amendment, which clearly allows for the free exercise of religion, medical emergency or not! For state and local officials to in effect dictate the practice (or non-practice) of religion dangerously treads on the US Constitution.

IS SECULAR HUMANISM A RELIGION? HOW DOES THIS CONNECT TO SOCIALISM?

Why does a consideration of secular humanism as a religion even matter? Surely, by its definition, secular

---

[1] Jefferson's Letter to the Danbury Baptists, January 1, 1802, Library of Congress, https://www.loc.gov/loc/lcib/9806/danpre.html.

humanism is secular and thus separate from the sacred. Case closed. Or is it?

First, the *Merriam-Webster Dictionary* defines *religion* as, among other things:

> "the service and worship of God or the supernatural";

> "commitment or devotion to religious faith or observance"; and

> "a personal set or institutionalized system of religious attitudes, beliefs, and practices."[2]

Secular humanism is a worldview or philosophy that rejects religious dogma as well as any belief in a supernatural higher power or person and rather embraces human reason, naturalism, and science as the basis for human morality and the issue of good and evil.

Historically, early proponents of humanism, such as John Dewey and Julian Huxley, spoke of their convictions in terms of "faith" and "religion." For about one hundred years, from 1875 on, it was common to speak of humanism as first outlined in the Humanist Manifesto of 1933 as the "new religion." In the United States humanists even sought tax exemption as a religious organization. In 1961 the US

---

2   Merriam-Webster.com, s.v. "religion," accessed June 9, 2020, https://www.merriam-webster.com/dictionary/religion.

Supreme Court referred to secular humanism as a "religion."[3]

Jewish Marxist academics who arrived in the United States after being thrown out of Germany by Hitler in the 1930s began to spread their deconstructionist ideas in leading colleges and universities, such as Berkeley, Brandeis, Princeton, and Columbia. They attacked basic Western values and practices: family, Christianity, capitalism, patriarchy, authority, patriotism, conservatism, and nationalism. They argued that children growing up in male-led, religious, and capitalistic societies would become racist and fascist. The solution to these problems, as they saw it, was to liberate women and create a matriarchal society. Erich Fromm led the way in this revolution, maintaining that male/female differences were the product of societal variances and not inherently sexual or gender driven.

In the twenty-first century, more than ever, it seems that the humanist revolution continues with the emasculation of the American male.

With secular humanism, nothing is absolute, only relative. There is no eternity; only the temporal matters. In this scheme of things, in the end nothing is immoral; even homosexuality and pedophilia are acceptable.

When Christians began to push back on the secular humanist agenda in education, they did so under the establishment clause, found in the First Amendment of the

---

[3] Torcaso v. Watkins, 367 U.S. 488 (1961).

Constitution, which forbade Congress from establishing a state religion. They argued that secular humanism was a religion, and thus it was unconstitutional for its tenets to be taught in school. The matter became legally controversial, so secular humanists rebranded their movement as being "scientifically" based, and not a matter of religion or faith.

In their early history, as the secular humanists made inroads into the education system in the US, it was convenient to operate as a religion to enjoy the benefits of the "freedom to exercise" side of the coin. When they were accused of pushing their agenda in the public education system, they claimed they were *not* a religion (despite Supreme Court rulings to the contrary that defined them as a religious group).

In time, the courts themselves became increasingly secularist, and often ruled against Christian attempts to get secular humanism out of schools (just as secular humanists had argued to get Judeo-Christian influence removed from schools). The courts argued that secular humanism was not a religion for "establishment clause purposes," and thus its advocates were free to continue promoting their agenda.

The secular humanist way of thinking has had an impact on understanding much of human existence: morality, ethics, politics, economics, race, sexuality and gender, education, biology, psychology, law, history, entertainment, media, history, even theology (think liberation theology). Today, if you oppose secular humanism in most if not all these areas, you are often identified as unscientific, bigoted, superstitious, and even, ironically, evil. A whole generation of leaders and influencers have grown up in the US under secular humanist influence in schools, colleges, and universities.

You could say that secular humanists see problems in the world through the lens of "given enough time and systemic change, we humans [without God] can solve everything." Socialism fits in here. Conversely, those who believe in God grapple with the same problems by appealing to their higher power—God—to give them the needed help and wisdom to get out of the mess they find themselves in.

Regarding the socialism/Communism of the twentieth century, Stalin, Mao, and Pol Pot were atheists connected to secular humanism. They were responsible for some of, if not the worst of, the mass crimes against humanity of that century.

Secular humanists and neo-Marxists were intent on totally transforming society. Herbert Marcuse of "Make love, not war" fame advocated a new kind of tolerance that did not tolerate anything that opposed his "pleasure principle," designed to free everyone from the enslavement of traditional morality. Others, including Saul Alinsky, advocated the formation of alliances between minorities, feminists, environmentalists, gays, and transvestites. Alinsky called for "community organizing" to play its part in pressing for power in all forms and levels of government. He influenced such well-known left-of-center personages as Ralph Nader, Jesse Jackson, César Chávez, Hillary Clinton, and Barack Obama. His *Rules for Radicals* listed rules for socialist agitators to use for toppling the status quo.

AGENDA

Increasingly, secular humanists have seen science to be the panacea for all ills. Yet if you are honest, science has time and again shown itself to fall short of solving life's complexities. For example, scientists have still not been able to find a cure for the common cold.

Today, if you dare disagree with the philosophical currents of the day, you could be labeled a science "denier" in a nanosecond and subjected to ridicule that ironically reaches religious proportions. Oppose the radical feminist agenda and you are labeled a "sexist." Stand for secure borders and you are "xenophobic."

In many universities today, reasonable, and civil debate between those holding opposing views is swamped by partisan toxicity. Many universities that are supposedly committed to "unity through diversity" regularly ban conservative speakers from their campuses and even coddle their students in "safe spaces," all the while indoctrinating young minds with secular humanism and socialism. This process churns out cookie-cutter modern socialists to a point where today 58 percent of eighteen- to thirty-four-year-olds see socialism as good for America.[4] In fact, in some circles,

---

4   Andrew O'Reilly, "New Group Launches to Warn Young People about Socialism," Fox News, August 25, 2019, https://www.foxnews.com/politics/new-group-young-people-socialism.

it is now "cool" to be a socialist.[5] Sadly, these folks totally ignore the scientific evidence of socialism's devastating failures before them.

---

5   Victor Davis Hanson, "Why Millennials See Destructive Socialism as Cool," *Washington Times*, November 6, 2019, https://www.washingtontimes.com/news/2019/nov/6/why-millennials-see-destructive-socialism-as-cool/.

8

POPULATION-GROWTH CONTROL

WHAT HAS THIS TO DO WITH SOCIALISM?

> *Then God blessed them, and God said to them, "Be fruitful and multiply; fill the earth and subdue it; have dominion over the fish of the sea, over the birds of the air, and over every living thing that moves on the earth."*
>
> —GENESIS 1:28

We all live on this planet and are not going anywhere soon in any great number, so any concern for our environment should be taken seriously.

Unfortunately, there is a lot of emotion, politics, and agenda-driven misinformation out there on the subjects of population and the environment. Surely, we should all be taking a deep breath and looking at the science on these matters rather than shouting at each other from behind our computers and banners on marches through the streets.

Three main groups of thinkers speak into the situation: (1) scientists who seem beholden to their sponsors to bend the data to fit desired results; (2) scientists who are skeptical of such an approach and prefer to stick to a long tradition of "impartial" scientific research and analysis; and (3) a composite of politicians, environmentalists, and media mouthpieces who more and more seem to be pursuing a globalist agenda, with its socialistic underpinnings. Of course, this last group invokes science to back their sociopolitical assertions, while demonizing anyone who dares to see things differently as ignorant at best or deniers at worst.

POPULATION GROWTH

Since Thomas Robert Malthus wrote his 1798 *Essay on the Principle of Population* presenting his theory of population growth and food production, there have been many clarion calls for controlling the number of people populating the planet. As population grows exponentially, food production does not—so Malthus's theory suggested. Sometime soon we will run out of the necessary resources (clean water, land, and food) to support ever-increasing large numbers of people.

Of course, there are blatant examples of environmental pollution (rivers, oceans, land), which are obviously caused by a poor understanding of our responsibility to carefully steward an integrated and finely tuned planetary ecology. But to go straight to controlling population growth through eugenics assumes that we know for sure that the planet cannot support projected increases in population.

When you honestly look at the projections made in the late 1960s and 1970s by scientists such as Paul R. Ehrlich of *The Population Bomb* fame, we see today a completely different picture. The world was going to end in 1985 through famine, starvation, disease, and sociopolitical upheaval if authorities did not take drastic action to curb population growth. The planet was even going to cool at an alarming rate, according to Professor Kenneth Watt of the University of California, by 2000.[1] The tune later changed when the focus shifted to CO_2 emissions and "global warming" because of the "greenhouse effect."

At that time (1968), the world's population was estimated at 3.7 billion. It grew to 4.8 billion in 1985 and as of July 2020 stood at approximately 7.8 billion.[2] Ehrlich's alarmism was quietly refuted, as world hunger declined by 216 million since 1992, world poverty fell from 60 percent to 9.6 percent in 2015, and world GDP/capita doubled from $5,165 in 1970 to $10,418 in 2015. Food production had grown exponentially, not linearly, as Malthus said, so worldwide population catastrophes did not occur.

---

1   See Maxim Lott, "Eight Botched Environmental Forecasts," Fox News, updated June 22, 2015, https://www.foxnews.com/science/eight-botched-environmental-forecasts.

2   "Current World Population," Worldometers, accessed July 22, 2020, https://www.worldometers.info/world-population/.

AGENDA

Since the '60s a series of agencies, including the Population Council, the World Bank, the United Nations Population Fund, and the International Planned Parenthood, have promoted sterilization and other approaches to curb growth. These included the infamous Communist Chinese one-child policy started in 1980 and then abandoned in 2015, mandated use of contraceptives, attaching health workers' salaries to the number of IUDs inserted into women, even sprinkling birth control pills via helicopter across rural villages.

To be fair, some agencies have sought to improve quality of life among poor people through sanitation, clean water, safe food supply, and education initiatives. These have over time served to lower birth rates (as parents saw that their kids were not dying off at such high rates as before). However, most population control efforts sponsored and supported by big government have their roots in the pseudo-science of *eugenics*, which was quite widespread in America and Europe in the first half of the twentieth century. This theory, like the Nazi program, called for selective breeding of humans to produce "better" and healthier people while sterilizing "undesirables." such as habitual criminals, those with disabilities, and even Jews and Gypsies.

THE EUGENICS MOVEMENT

The eugenics movement had its philosophical roots in Darwin's *On the Origin of Species* and Malthus's theory described in the previous section. The famously wealthy John

D. Rockefeller was exposed to these influences through professors at Brown University, such as Elisha Benjamin Andrews, and later by Sir Francis Galton, a Victorian scientist who was convinced humanity could be improved through selective breeding. Rockefeller set up "philanthropic" trusts, including the Rockefeller Institute for Medical Research (1901), which focused on the problem of overpopulation, especially among the lower classes of society. Margaret Sanger, the American birth control activist who opened the first birth control clinic in the US in 1916, had help from Rockefeller's lawyer in setting up the American Birth Control League, the forerunner of Planned Parenthood.

By the way, the playwright George Bernard Shaw called for government "death panels" to decide whether people should live or not.[3] He also supported eugenics, and even telephone inventor Alexander Graham Bell campaigned for the eradication of the "deaf race" through discouraging deaf people from marrying.[4]

The abortion industry in the United States was conveniently attached to a woman's rights to her "own body," and has tragically resulted in at least fifty million baby deaths

---

3   See "How Many People Have Been Put to Death as the Result of Darwin's Theory of Eugenics to Date?" yahoo answers, accessed June 18, 2020, https://answers.yahoo.com/question/index?qid=20110110124911AAvADdQ.

4   See "Signing, Alexander Graham Bell and the NAD," *Through Deaf Eyes*, March 2007, http://www.pbs.org/weta/throughdeafeyes/deaflife/bell_nad.html.

since the *Roe v. Wade* decision by the Supreme Court in 1973. (This decision ignored the rights of unborn babies, who were conveniently renamed "fetal tissue," eliminating their humanity.) This dehumanization of the babies served to minimize the horror of what has really been going on in what has become a multibillion-dollar "industry."

Thankfully, the development of ultrasound technology has helped mothers considering abortion to see what's really going on in their wombs, and many testimonies of children who have survived the abortion holocaust have given further impetus to a growing reaction to the barbaric practice of abortion.

Think of it: you and I and every single person alive today, including abortion advocates, are products of a pro-life choice by our mothers to go through with the pregnancy. Just saying.

Interestingly, Margaret Sanger, the infamous eugenicist of the early twentieth century, and Microsoft founder/philanthropist Bill Gates have a connection: the promotion of eugenics.

Sanger, as founder of the Birth Control League (again, the future Planned Parenthood), strongly advocated for compulsory sterilization of those who were physically or mentally disabled, as well as the segregation of illiterates, paupers, unemployables, criminals, prostitutes, and drug addicts into state work camps. They could be returned to society if they underwent sterilization after showing good behavior. Sanger's segregationist ideas included race: the "negro" was to be kept unenlightened to the fact that her programs would foster a significant decrease in the numbers of their population, so she encouraged the help of religious ministers to quash any such idea. Her defenders argue that she was not advocating a racial component to her birth control measures, while her detractors disagree. The "Negro Project," as she called it, was supposedly intended to integrate medically supervised birth control, including abortion, into public health services to improve the general welfare of the Negro.

She even proudly addressed the women of the Ku Klux Klan in 1926 with her ideas. The Klan was in those days solidly in the camp of the Democratic Party, which incidentally was still split over the issue of slavery, while Republicans had already settled on abolition. Margaret Sanger also showed socialist leanings in her writings and associations. She was part of the New York Socialist Party taking part in leftist labor actions. It can be argued that her ideas on women's freedom and empowerment played a significant role in the history of a woman's "right to choose."

A couple of statistics today provide an interesting perspective. Seventy-nine percent of Planned Parenthood abortion clinics are within walking distance of predominantly African American and Latino-dominated neighborhoods.[5] Thus, the abortion rate among African Americans

---

5   Catherine Davis and Bradley Mattes, "Abortion's Twisted Logic of Racism during Black History Month," *Washington Examiner*, February 28, 2020, https://www.washingtonexaminer.com/opinion/op-eds/since-roe-abortion-has-killed-more-black-babies-than-the-entire-black-population-of-the-u-s-in-1960.

is disproportionately high: they account for 36 percent of all abortions even though they comprise just over 13 percent of the total US population.[6] Abortion seemingly has a racial component to it.

Back in the 1920s and 1930s, eugenics (the practice of selectively breeding human populations through birth control and even sterilization to improve the population's gene pool) enjoyed wide support from doctors, scientists, and the general public in the US. Margaret Sanger printed many articles supporting eugenics during that time.

Sanger's movement impacted many nations, including India, Singapore, Japan, China, Korea, and much of Europe. Sterilization-of-the-unfit programs were adopted by so-called progressive western Nordic countries, such as Sweden, Norway, Finland, Denmark, and most infamously, Nazi Germany. Yes, Nazi Germany, which incidentally had close ties with American eugenicist scientists concentrated largely in California, of all places. California's history of eugenics is less than stellar. Hitler studied American eugenics laws of the various states that adopted them, including California. He then quoted American eugenic ideology in *Mein Kampf* (published in 1924), claiming science validated his points of view. Hitler tried to medicalize his rampant anti-Semitism

---

6   Emily Ward, "CDC: 36% of Abortions Abort Black Babies," CNSNews, November 28, 2018, https://www.cnsnews.com/news/article/emily-ward/blacks-make-134-population-36-abortions.

by using the observations of pseudoscientific eugenics.[7]

At the height of the movement in the first half of the twentieth century, thirty states had laws on their books regarding eugenic practices. California was the epicenter of the American eugenics movement, which enjoyed significant funding from the Rockefeller Foundation, the Carnegie Institution, and the Harriman Railroad empire. Scientists from such respected universities as Harvard, Yale, Stanford, and Princeton championed race theory and race science. According to Edwin Black, *SFGATE* contributor and author of *IBM and the Holocaust*, "the Rockefeller Foundation helped found the German eugenics program and even funded the program that Josef Mengele worked in before he went to Auschwitz" to perform his deadly experiments on camp internees, mostly Jews.[8] Mengele, whose byname was "Angel of Death," was also part of a team of German doctors who selected victims for the gas chambers.[9]

Remember: the Nazis were National Socialists.

Fortunately, after the exposure of World War II holocaust atrocities, eugenics was declared a crime against humanity, and the movement in its rawest expressions lost momentum.

---

7   Edwin Black, "Eugenics and the Nazis—the California Connection," *SFGATE*, November 9, 2003, https://www.sfgate.com/opinion/article/Eugenics-and-the-Nazis-the-California-2549771.php.

8   Black.

9   The Editors of *Encyclopaedia Britannica*, "Josef Mengele," Britannica, accessed June 10, 2020, https://www.britannica.com/biography/Josef-Mengele.

On to Bill Gates and his connection to eugenics in more detail. Gates, the computer whiz kid who founded Microsoft along with Paul Allen, went on to become, for a time, the richest man in the world, according to *Forbes*.[10] In 2000, he and his wife, Melinda, launched a philanthropic foundation based in Seattle, Washington, called the Bill & Melinda Gates Foundation.

The Gates Foundation has donated billions of dollars to the cause of improving global health, largely by sponsoring vaccine and agricultural programs in underdeveloped Third World countries. Bill Jr. was motivated by the marriage of information and medical technology, especially as it related to population growth problems and "reproductive health," which has become euphemistic jargon for birth control measures such as sterilization and abortion. His father, William Gates Sr., was at one time head of Planned Parenthood. It seems as if eugenics runs in the family.

Ironically, Bill Jr. has a strong conviction that improving health care, primarily through vaccines (and other measures, such as sanitation and clean water programs) would achieve population control and thus eventual sustainability of the planet. Of course, scientific research does show that when a society increases in disposable wealth beyond survival, as well as in education, health, and welfare, they tend to have fewer children over time. The "better off" you are, the fewer

---

10   Luisa Kroll, "Forbes 2017 Billionaires List: Meet the Richest People on the Planet," *Forbes*, 2017.

children you have, since more survive to adulthood than die off in infancy and early childhood.

Gates has worked closely over the years with UNICEF (United Nations Children's Fund) and WHO (World Health Organization) using vaccines to combat tetanus in Africa. One vaccine, however, is under suspicion of being tainted with hCG, a contraceptive hormone. Some argue this has amounted to a sophisticated approach to reduce the number of pregnancies. Bill Gates has become a leading voice at the forefront of the coronavirus event of late 2019 and 2020 that has altered the world as it was known—at least for now (July 2020).

WHO's director-general, Tedros Adhonum Ghebreyesus of Ethiopia, declared on April 4, 2020, that abortion was an essential service during the COVID-19 pandemic. "Sexual and reproductive health care is integral to universal health coverage and achieving the right to health," he said in his public statement.[11] This on the heels of many states in the US declaring that abortions were "essential services" during the shutdowns/lockdowns across the country. Incidentally, WHO has been criticized for its initial failure to declare the virus a public health emergency at the outset of the outbreak. It took them at

---

11 See Devrupa Rakshit, "WHO: Abortion Is an Essential Healthcare Service During Covid19 Pandemic," *Swaddle*, April 13, 2020, https://theswaddle.com/who-classifies-abortion-as-essential-healthcare-service-during-covid19-pandemic/.

least a month to take any action in seeming deference to China. Director-general Tedros pushed back against this criticism by crying racism and declared that he was "proud of being black or proud of being negro," as he put it.[12]

Interestingly, the Gates Foundation has funded the UK's Pirbright Institute, a world-leading research and surveillance center targeting viral diseases of animals and viruses that spread from animals to humans, with $5.5 million. The institute had filed a patent for a live attenuated corona-type virus to be used in the production of vaccines, claiming their patents pertain only to animals, not to humans.

Now, let us dig deeper into the coronavirus event itself, an event that took most by surprise . . . but not all.

---

12 Agnès Pedrero, "WHO Chief Tedros in the Eye of Pandemic and Trump Storm," Yahoo! News, April 15, 2020, https://news.yahoo.com/chief-tedros-eye-pandemic-trump-storm-204356689.html.

9

THE CORONAVIRUS 2019/2020 EVENT

CONNECTING THE DOTS

You shall not be afraid of the terror by night,
Nor of the arrow that flies by day,
Nor of the pestilence that walks in darkness,
Nor of the destruction that lays waste at noonday.

—PSALM 91:5-6

Back in March 2015 at a TED talk conference, Bill Gates essentially predicted that a viral worldwide pandemic was a greater likelihood of danger to mankind than, for example, nuclear war. He argued that we spend far too little on averting a pandemic that could medically impact up to three billion people, with huge economic consequences too. In Gates's understanding worldwide vaccines are a key component in world health or control, so much so that way back in 2010 he kicked off a "decade of vaccines" with a pledged donation of $10 billion to research and develop the needed serums. "We've made vaccines our number-one priority at the Gates Foundation," he said in January 2010. A large portion of Gates's money has gone to GAVI, the Global Alliance for Vaccines and Immunization.[1]

In May 2010, the Rockefeller Foundation and Global Business Network published a white paper innocently called "Scenarios for the Future of Technology and International Development," outlining a planned scenario in which governments would be able to more easily control society by locking down the population in a contrived pandemic. It was dubbed "Lock Step" since tighter top-down authoritarian control of citizens is facilitated through such an event.[2]

In October 2019 at the Bloomberg School of Public Health in New York, New York, the Gates Foundation cohosted with the John Hopkins Center for Health Security and the World Economic Forum a high-level pandemic exercise named "Event 201." It involved discussions about how government and private partnerships would

---

[1] Post Staff Report, "Bill Gates Donates $10B for Vaccines," *New York Post*, January 29, 2010, https://nypost.com/2010/01/29/bill-gates-donates-10b-for-vaccines/.

[2] See the Rockefeller Foundation and Global Business Network, "Scenarios for the Future of Technology and International Development," May 2010, at https://www.nommeraadio.ee/meedia/pdf/RRS/Rockefeller%20Foundation.pdf, esp. 18–25.

be necessary to properly respond to a severe pandemic to diminish large-scale societal and economic consequences. Coincidence perhaps? Time will tell, hopefully.

Organizers of Event 201 stated that they had "modeled a fictional coronavirus pandemic," adding, "we explicitly stated that it was not a prediction" of infection cases. Their statement referred to the fictional virus as a "mock novel coronavirus."[3]

Furthermore, there are close links with Bill Gates and GlaxoSmithKline (GSK), the British multinational corporation that produces vaccines. Incidentally, GSK has an agreement with the giant Chinese-based Clover Biopharmaceutical for the distribution of the antidote/vaccine against COVID-19 as soon as it is available. How convenient. Perhaps a case of "create a problem, have a solution ready" . . . and make lots of money in the process too?

Vaccines are big on Gates's agenda to help especially the poorer nations in the world. He calls for vaccines to be quickly produced at low cost in great quantities; in fact, he has the whole world in mind. In a Fox News interview with Chris Wallace, aired on April 5, 2020, he made just such a push. He advocates helping these nations develop more robust health systems in their countries and greater

---

[3] John Hopkins Bloomberg School of Public Health, Center for Health Security, "Statement about nCoV and Our Pandemic Exercise," accessed June 10, 2020, https://www.centerforhealthsecurity.org/news/center-news/2020-01-24-Statement-of-Clarification-Event201.html.

cross-border cooperation between nations. Richer nations should help finance such endeavors.

It takes a good crisis in the West to motivate the West to do something—that is, to get government and private agencies/businesses involved to produce a vaccine to be used everywhere. Recently, the Gates Foundation has pledged $100 million in the effort to address the coronavirus 2019 pandemic.[4] Sounds all well and good, philanthropically speaking, but the Gates Foundation connections with Big Pharma companies such as Merck, Johnson & Johnson, Roche, Pfizer, Novartis, and GlaxoSmithKline (GDSK) must be viewed with concern.

Today, vaccine development has become a bigger and bigger money spinner in contrast to the profit margins in prescription drug production, which have, year after year, decreased in the last decade. Drug companies have been losing billions due to lawsuits for damages from drug side effects.

The coronavirus event of 2019/2020 has seen Bill Gates pushing for worldwide vaccination, with a call for a digital "certificate" of proof of such vaccination to open travel around the world.[5] Such surveillance is seen by some as part

---

[4] AFP, "Gates Foundation Announces $100 Million for Coronavirus Response," msn, February 5, 2020, https://www.msn.com/en-us/health/health-news/gates-foundation-announces-dollar100-million-for-coronavirus-response/ar-BBZGdMx.

[5] Devin Coldewey, "Bill Gates Addresses Coronavirus Fears and Hopes in AMA," TechCrunch, March 18, 2020, https://techcrunch.com/2020/03/18/bill-gates-addresses-coronavirus-fears-and-hopes-in-ama/.

of the globalist agenda to control world population even more in these days of high technology. As poorer people in developing countries around the world are gaining greater and greater access to wireless smartphones, some argue that these phones are to be used to surveil/track the population regarding medical matters, such as vaccines. Movement and travel can be controlled by means of such tracking. For Gates, privacy concerns are a small price to pay in stopping pandemics with vaccines.

Promoting a "digital ID" for medical purposes (as opposed to archaic paper documentation) is an important cog in facilitating the United Nations Agenda 2030's seventeen "sustainable development" goals. Here we start to see how the dots connect with globalism and socialism.

ID 2020 is an alliance of public-private partners, including the UN, Microsoft, Accenture, the Rockefeller Foundation, and GAVI, partly funded by the Gates Foundation to the tune of at least $4.51 billion by 2020.

The key goal of ID 2020 is an electronic ID program that uses generalized vaccination as a platform for digital identity for everyone on the planet. Access to such reliable digital IDs, especially for poorer folk in developing nations, is now considered a "universal human right" according to the manifesto of ID 2020.[6] Various technologies, from smartphone apps and implanted chips to nano-implantation of tattoo-like

---

6   The Alliance Manifesto, ID 2020 website, accessed June 18, 2020, https://id2020.org/manifesto.

material are being developed and beta tested right now.

The official rationale is to make ID more efficient across states, nations, and then the world. Tracking of infections, vaccinations, and even finances, can be facilitated through digital ID. Some argue that a sinister by-product of this is another layer of control and surveillance of anyone and everyone. This control is part of the New World Order.

According to various media reports, China is already tracking its citizens through a smartphone app in the Wuhan province. South Korea has also tracked its COVID-19 quarantined citizens using smartphones. Israel approved emergency measures to use smartphone technology to track people infected with COVID-19 and those quarantined. The concerns of privacy advocates are being drowned out by calls to stop the spread and get real-time data so as not to lag behind in testing in any area.

Regarding the vaccines themselves, the concern goes so far as to question whether the genetic alteration of RNA being built into the COVID-19 vaccine is part of an extremely dangerous trend not commonly known at this point. Mandatory vaccination with a one-size-fits-all approach is seen by Gates as vital in reducing CO_2 levels worldwide. In his TED talk, Gates made the connection between worldwide population control and climate change clear. His equation showed essentially that to reduce the human influence on the increase of CO_2, we must reduce the number of humans, and that is achieved largely in his plan through vaccines.

Gates, along with Dr. Deborah Birx and Dr. Tony Fauci

(members of the US COVID-19 task force to fight the virus under President Trump and Vice President Mike Pence) pushed back on data showing the efficacy of the remedial or therapeutic use of hydroxychloroquine (a previously tested anti-malaria drug used by doctors around the world). Dr Fauci argued that any reported positive outcomes were "anecdotal" and thus not reliable, scientifically. He spoke of "double blind" studies that still needed to be conducted on hydroxychloroquine's efficacy. Perhaps he forgot that back in 2005 a version of the drug had already been studied and found to be useful as a therapeutic drug in combating viral infections from the same family of coronaviruses as the virus affecting people today.[7]

The study was published in *Virology*, the journal of his own NIAID (National Institute of Infectious Diseases) and showed that the SARS-Cov-1 virus studied shared 79 percent of the genome of today's "novel" coronavirus 2.[8]

By the way, Dr. Fauci, entrenched as head of NIAID for thirty-six years, touted the expensive drug Remdesivir—a failed Ebola antiviral drug from a few years ago—in place of the cheap by comparison hydroxychloroquine (which

---

[7] See James Delingpole, "Delingpole: Chloroquine Known as Effective Against Coronavirus Since 2005," Breitbart, March 10, 2020, https://www.breitbart.com/politics/2020/03/19/chloroquine-known-as-effective-against-coronavirus-since-2005/.

[8] See Dale Fisher and David Heymann, "Q&A: The Novel Coronavirus Outbreak Causing COVID-19," *BMC Medicine* 18, no. 57 (2020), https://bmcmedicine.biomedcentral.com/articles/10.1186/s12916-020-01533-w.

to date has relatively few serious side effects when used on COVID-19 patients). In addition, Fauci's NIAID is working closely with the pharma company Gilead to conduct phase II human trials on Remdesivir. Side effects of the drug are respiratory failure and organ impairment. Not good. So far, early tests on humans have shown little efficacy of the drug as a therapeutic.

Leaders such as Governor Cuomo from New York have been slow to release hydroxychloroquine for COVID-19 treatment, despite its safe use under doctor's orders. Some commentators have argued that the slow adoption of this drug by authorities was politically motivated against the Trump administration.

Also, in April 2020, TV's Dr. Oz was interviewed on TV, where he shared that research suggests a strong connection between the use of hydroxychloroquine by lupus patients and a low incidence of COVID-19 infections in that group.[9]

It appears that the drug used for more than fifty years with very few serious side effects may indeed be a useful and cheap prophylaxis or preventative drug. Subsequent to this quite some pushback has occurred on the efficacy and safety of the very cheap drug hydroxychloroquine. One can only wonder why, when the drug has safely been used for so long.

---

9   See Melanie Arter, "Dr. Oz: Complications from Hydroxychloroquine Were 'Trivial Like Rashes,'" Cnsnews, April 8, 2020, https://www.cnsnews.com/article/national/melanie-arter/dr-oz-complications-hydroxychloroquine-were-trivial-rashes.

Dr. Birx (who reached the rank of colonel in the US military and is the coordinator of the United States Government Activities to Combat HIV/AIDS and U.S. special representative for global health diplomacy), Dr. Fauci, and other epidemiologists have used a model of pandemic prediction produced by IHME (the Institute for Health Metrics and Evaluation) at UW Medicine in Washington State. The Bill & Melinda Gates Foundation is one of the core funders of IHME, donating millions to the organization to develop predictive models.

According to media coverage where the COVID-19 US task force led by Vice President Pence presented its daily briefings to the nation, this model was used to promote lockdowns of whole regions and even nations worldwide till the vaccines can be developed and tested. The model initially predicted 1–2 million deaths in the US, which Drs. Fauci and Birx downgraded to between 100,000 and 200,000 at the end of March 2020. In early April, they lowered the number to 60,000 deaths, supposedly based on actual data coming in from around the country rather than on modeling assumptions. At the beginning of April 2020, pushback against official modeling projections began receiving more and more media coverage.

Alex Berenson, a journalist who used to work for the *New York Times*, and is now presumably free from their leftist editorial policies and agendas, argued that the models were deeply flawed in that they factored in such things as social distancing and other mitigating measures from the start, yet still came up with the huge numbers referenced above. The success of these mitigating measures has been declared to be the reason why actual data put into the Washington model later moved the modeling numbers downward. Oh well.

As the numbers rolled in from around the country, the pressure to "do something" may have driven state governors and local county officials and mayors to outdo each other in the scramble to avoid swamping the health and hospital systems and save lives.

Interestingly, COVID-19 death figures are derived from recording hospital cases where a person dies with the coronavirus infection in his or her body. These death numbers *do not* explicitly show to what extent the virus itself caused the recorded death. Underlying conditions (maladies that make a person's immune system weak and more susceptible to complications) such as diabetes, congestive heart failure, and other lung issues caused by smoking and so on, are *not* singled out in the records.

So, COVID-19 could be the major cause of death, or merely a contributing factor, or even just simply present when someone was dying anyway. The numbers put out to the public do not show any such critical distinction. The lines have been so blurred that they cannot possibly be purely scientific, and certainly should not have been used to make major policy decisions.

Get this: Doctors were even officially guided by NVSS, or the National Vital Statistics System, which is part of the

CDC, or Centers for Disease Control, to make "judgment" calls on a patient's death even where no COVID-19 testing has been done. They were to report the underlying cause of death as due to COVID-19 and not any preexisting serious life-threatening conditions, like COPD, emphysema, diabetes, and so on.[10]

Two statements by Dr. Birx recorded on national TV during the daily task force briefings in April 2020 are quite revealing. She said, "We've taken a very liberal approach to mortality." She went on to say, "If someone dies *with* COVID-19, we are counting that *as a COVID-19 death*."[11]

In my view, the death count from COVID-19 alone could be off by as much as 40 percent!

According to Senator Scott Jensen from Minnesota when interviewed on Fox, hospitals get paid $13,000 by Medicare when they admit a COVID-19 patient, and even more ($39,000) if that patient goes on a ventilator.[12] This is happening while hospitals have been forced to stop elective surgery, and doctors, nurses, and other health care workers are being laid off because of this curtailment.

---

10 See NVSS, "Guidance for Certifying Deaths Due to Coronavirus Disease 2019 (COVID–19)," *Vital Statistics Reporting Guidance*, report no. 3 (April 2020), https://www.cdc.gov/nchs/data/nvss/vsrg/vsrg03-508.pdf.

11 Dr. Deborah Birx, in a YouTube video of a White House COVID-19 task force briefing, April 8, 2020, https://www.youtube.com/watch?v=JKlYr-ZM_d8.

12 "Dr Scott Jensen on Broad Covid-19 Death Count Guidelines & Financial Incentives," YouTube video, Fox News Alert posted April 10, 2020, by Giulio Col, https://www.youtube.com/watch?v=AR2fY7dVdMo.

AGENDA

Follow the money in all this and you might begin to understand what is happening.

In Italy, where COVID-19 death rates were high compared to nations around the world (in the top three in Europe per capita—WHO data), the general population is older, and thus more susceptible to infectious disease. Then too, a flu vaccine was introduced and promoted there in early 2019 (before the COVID-19 outbreak). This vaccine had four untested strains in it that included the highly pathogenic H1N1 virus. It has been postulated that the immune system of the general population in Italy was already weakened by the previous vaccine and the people who took it in early 2019 were more susceptible to COVID-19 infection in late 2019 and early 2020.

In late April 2020, Denmark passed legislation that allows for mandatory vaccination for COVID-19 till March 2021. It also allows for citizens who refuse testing for COVID-19 to face fines and potential prison time. These people will also be prevented from shopping and even from entering grocery stores, public institutions, and hospitals. Public transport is also off-limits to these lawbreakers, who will be tracked. All in the name of a medical emergency that you dare not question for fear of being called a conspiracy theorist and accused of being "anti-science."

This is a where modern authoritarian top-down "democratic" dictatorship fits in with socialism's goal of strong central government involvement in all of the affairs of citizens.

As of April 30, 2020, Denmark had only had 452

COVID-19-related deaths out of 9,158 reported cases in a national total of 5,792,202, yet it passed this draconian-type legislation, which, to some, amounts to "medical martial law."[13]

Moderna Therapeutics is a company currently working on a coronavirus vaccine. It has in the past received a grant of $20 million from the Bill & Melinda Gates Foundation for RNA-based therapeutics geared toward preventing HIV infection. This genetic technology is being used to develop the coronavirus vaccine. Gates said in April 2020 that seven companies he is funding were working side by side researching a COVID-19 vaccine, of which only two are likely in the end to be acceptable. Besides Moderna, Inovio Pharmaceuticals is also working on a vaccine and has received funding from the Gates Foundation.

Gates has said that he is prepared to spend (or, lose) billions in the race to fast-track and test the vaccines.[14] He wants production to be ramped up from millions of doses to billions in order to vaccinate everyone on the planet that can be reached to protect us from a virus that so far has killed fewer than the number of deaths from the annual flu.

---

13 See Insight History, "Video: Medical Martial Law and the Nuremberg Code in the Age of COVID-19," Global Research, March 25, 2020, https://www.globalresearch.ca/medical-martial-law-nuremberg-code-age-covid-19/5707483.

14 See Jennifer Calfas, "Bill Gates to Help Fund Coronavirus-Vaccine Development," *Wall Street Journal*, April 5, 2020, https://www.wsj.com/articles/bill-gates-to-spend-billions-on-coronavirus-vaccine-development-11586124716.

AGENDA

Total world population number control (or more accurately, decrease) through vaccinations, and woman's reproductive health initiatives (aka abortion and contraception) is the goal. Long-term "sustainability" on the local, national, and global levels is supposed to make all such measures palatable.

As in any field of endeavor, but especially in medicine, honesty and integrity should be highly valued. After all, lives are at stake. Increasingly, people are waking up to the information/disinformation war between China and the US over the COVID-19 event of 2019/2020. Sadly, Chinese doctor Li Wenliang in Wuhan, who tried to warn the world in the early stages of the outbreak there, died. He was thirty-four. Li was warned by the authorities not to "disturb the social order" and "spread rumors to his colleagues" about protecting themselves against a viral outbreak he saw occurring. Eight other doctors working in the area were also investigated by the Chinese authorities for spreading rumors at a critical time in the outbreak. Had the information been released early on, many lives could have been saved. In viral outbreaks, early communication and cooperation have a significant effect on the containment of any spreading.

Some statistics from late 2019 and early 2020 simply do not add up: like the number of deaths versus the number of cases in mainland China. These were reported as being extremely low in comparison to total population numbers there. But then, information flow in China, especially through the internet, is centrally controlled or censored by the Communist Party–controlled authorities.

If you believe that the mainstream media in the US does not put a spin on what is put out, then it is time to start looking at things more carefully.

Disease surveillance worldwide plays into generally shared medical safety concerns, but also into a broader picture of global cooperation. Global cooperation is hard to oppose; it seems so obvious to coordinate efforts to stem any viral outbreaks on a worldwide basis. We live in such a connected world with international travel and trade. However, even the scientists and health officials we have had to listen to, have an agenda. What is their worldview and political ideology? Does this impact their so-called scientific objectivity? Obviously, we must guard against cynicism, and always mistrusting those in authority, but at the same time we cannot afford to be naive.

For example, WHO director-general Tedros Adhanom Ghebreyesus, mentioned earlier, hails from Ethiopia, a socialist state, where he previously served that government as minister of health from 2005 to 2012 and later as minister of foreign affairs from 2012 to 2016. He is not from a medical background, let alone an MD, but is an academic and politician who has advocated for policies that smack of socialism to improve life in Africa.

Tedros is implicated in a cover-up of the mishandling and information suppression associated with three possible cholera epidemics in Ethiopia in 2006, 2009, and 2011. Of course, these allegations are denied as a smear campaign that took place before his election in May 2017 as WHO director-general.

Most recently, he has been criticized for his overt praise of China's efforts to contain the coronavirus outbreak, which some argue has not been accurately reported in the light of China's actions to suppress information flows, both within China itself (censorship) and to the rest of the world. Perspective and truth telling are needed but probably not forthcoming—at least as yet.

Notably, Ethiopia has historically been a Marxist-Leninist one-party communist state, which from 1987 to 1991 employed, among other measures, "land reform" strategies that may well have exacerbated severe famine issues in that land. Most recently, after conflict both within the state and with its neighbors, efforts have been made to denationalize some state-owned enterprises. Today, Ethiopia, with its somewhat mixed economy, is still classified as a socialist state.

THE REOPENING OF THE US ECONOMY FROM LATE APRIL 2020 ON

"We can't have the cure be worse than the problem," quipped President Donald Trump in March 2020.[15] And indeed, the longer the coronavirus mitigation efforts by the various states continued, the worse the economic outlook. Millions

---

15 Jill Colvin, Josh Boak, and Ricardo Alonso-Zaldivar, "Trump: 'We Can't Have the Cure Be Worse Than the Problem,'" RealClear Politics, March 24, 2020, https://www.realclearpolitics.com/articles/2020/03/24/trump_we_cant_have_the_cure_be_worse_than_the_problem_142750.html.

of working people, still out of work, are now waiting for their stimulus checks. Street and vehicular protests against overreach by some governors began to pop up in mid-April 2020. This was spurred on by more and more information coming out that pointed to how statistics were used to set lockdown policies in place. There were no consistent baselines to compare local, state, national, and indeed, international statistics. Changes in reporting guidelines happened from one week to the next. For example, New York State case numbers (and deaths to COVID-19) jumped significantly when testing became more widely available. The spike in the graphs did *not* on its own show actual new cases, and thus a deepening of the crisis, but only reflected the jump due to more accurate testing results.

Those who bought into the narrative being communicated by the authorities easily agreed to the notion of taking people's temperatures at checkpoints and even business entrances. Tracking and monitoring of people who had had COVID-19 and had developed immunity was suggested. "Testing, testing, testing" was the cry.

Let us investigate the testing issue for the COVID-19 event. If you have people dying from a disease like COVID-19 without testing, you have little idea of what strategy to follow to deal with the problem. The more you test, the more you know what you are dealing with, that is, if the tests are carefully administered to prevent false positives. You do not want to count false positive results and make policy decisions based on numbers that include these. Then consider this: What about the people who were infected but showed no major symptoms to initiate any test and are now well? How many of them are out there in society to serve as a base denominator to the numerator?

You therefore need reliable antibody tests to show the number of people currently infected against the total number of people who have been infected. In this way you get a better perspective of how serious the outbreak really is, and hopefully you then do not overreact.

Dr. Jay Bhattacharya of Stanford along with a team of co-researchers did such an antibody study in April 2020 in Santa Clara County, California, and found that "the population-weighted prevalence [of antibodies] was 2.81%." This "implies that the infection is much more widespread than indicated by the number of confirmed cases" (as reported to the CDC).[16]

In short, the research showed that there were between fifty and eighty times more people that already had COVID-19, than the official figure. That means the authority's modeling of the spread, and then the official testing (using the RTPCR test), was way off in its sequencing and significance. The mitigation efforts, which involved the lockdowns, social distancing, and so forth, can therefore be seen in a whole new light. It is not unreasonable to conclude that

---

16   Eran Bendavid et al., "COVID-19 Antibody Seroprevalence in Santa Clara County, California," medRxiv, April 30, 2020, https://www.medrxiv.org/content/10.1101/2020.04.14.20062463v2.

governmental reactions need not have been nearly as severe as they were.

The antibody-based test results in Santa Clara County show that COVID-19 is *not* as deadly as was initially thought. In fact, it is argued that COVID-19 is about as deadly as the seasonal flu, with a mortality rate of 0.1 percent or maybe 0.2 percent. Dr. Fauci said in late March 2020 that the COVID-19 mortality rate was ten times that of the seasonal flu! I guess he was basing it on data he had at that time and the modeling he trusted. Remember: he is a scientist, and science must never be questioned, right?

Another antibody study in Los Angeles County, with its ten million population, has been conducted with similar findings—up to fifty-five times more cases of people with antibodies than the "official" numbers have shown so far. That is 4.1 percent of adults in the county! The mortality rate therefore drops significantly to below 1 percent. Once again, severe lockdown policies have been followed based on the extremely limited data of hospital-related tests and COVID-19 deaths only. As of April 28, 2020, only one thousand deaths were reported in LA County.[17]

On April 23, 2020, New York State reported on a statewide study using a sample of three thousand subjects

---

[17] See Gennady Sheyner, "Los Angeles Study Backs Stanford Researchers' Conclusion about High Prevalence of COVID-19," Palo Alto Online, April 21, 2020, https://www.paloaltoonline.com/news/2020/04/21/los-angeles-study-backs-stanford-researchers-conclusion-about-high-prevalence-of-covid-19.

in nineteen counties and forty localities with COVID-19 antibodies (meaning they have had the infection and recovered). The statistics showed that 13.9 percent were positive for the antibodies, which equates to 2.7 million people in the state—much more than the numbers used before in modeling that drove the lockdown and other mitigation measures. The mortality rate in this study dropped down to 0.5 percent from 5 percent![18]

When broken down into a New York City split within the state, it showed a similar pattern. Thankfully, the more data that comes available, the less sensational the analysis of the event has looked, and sadly, the more draconian the lockdown measures appear to be.

Yet another antibody study conducted by the Stanford research team, this time with Major League Baseball employees across twenty-seven teams nationwide, shows fewer infections than expected (under 1 percent), with a mortality rate of zero, which is good news. The sampling demographic may have had an impact on the results compared to stats from various parts of the country. The employees tested tended to be younger, with fewer existing comorbidities, and they had started earlier than most in the US in their use of personal protection equipment. This

---

18 See Noah Higgins-Dunn, "New York Antibody Study Estimates 13% of Residents Have Had the Coronavirus, CNBC, April 23, 2020, https://www.cnbc.com/2020/04/23/new-york-antibody-study-estimates-13point9percent-of-residents-have-had-the-coronavirus-cuomo-says.html.

result came out on May 10, 2020.[19]

Back to Santa Clara County, California, with its two million citizens, to "contact trace" the fifty to eighty thousand people who are likely to have COVID-19 antibodies in their system will be an almost impossible task requiring an army of investigators. This is precisely what California governor Gavin Newson put forward when he said the state would use and drastically expand existing infectious disease contact tracing systems.[20] Let us see how that plays out in practice.

Viral infection is just one of the risks of living in an interconnected world where people travel all over the place all the time, spreading germs, bacteria, and viruses. Even with the development of a vaccine that is intended for worldwide application, it is simply not possible to eradicate the virus and any other future strain that may develop. Then, conclusively no amount of surveillance, testing, and mitigating efforts will stop everything in its tracks. Yet it appears as if some in authority are saying, "We will give it our best shot"—with smartphone app tracing, camera surveillance,

---

19   See Jasmine Kerber, "Stanford Researchers Test MLB Employees for COVID-19 Antibodies," *Stanford Daily*, April 30, 2020, https://www.stanforddaily.com/2020/04/30/stanford-researchers-test-mlb-employees-for-covid-19-antibodies/.

20   See "Governor Newsom Launches California Connected—California's Contact Tracing Program and Public Awareness Campaign," Office of Governor Gavin Newsom, May 22, 2020, https://www.gov.ca.gov/2020/05/22/governor-newsom-launches-california-connected-californias-contact-tracing-program-and-public-awareness-campaign/.

home inspections, and other interventions, such as chip implantation and nano injection technology.

Authoritarian overreach and the agenda behind the efforts to stop the "silent enemy" must be viewed with extreme caution. The fact that just about the whole world got on board with severe mitigation efforts in a matter of weeks only points to a unique level of agreement never seen before. This is a connecting mindset that drives this.

Some underplay the importance of these antibody test studies, saying they indicate that we are nowhere near "herd immunity" percentages—anywhere between 60 and 70 percent of the population (more on herd immunity later). YouTube even took down posts made by other medical doctors from Bakersfield, California, where they discussed their findings on antibody testing they had done. They opined that the death rates in their area should be dramatically reduced to below 1 percent and argued that this more accurate rate should be fed into the decision-making process in California's reopening of the economy from the lockdown there.[21]

YouTube's actions are likened to blatant censorship of free speech, something that is right up the socialist street of top-down control and manipulation. YouTube's CEO,

---

21 See "Elon Musk Blasts YouTube for Banning Californian Doctors' Video That Claimed Physicians Are Being Pressurized into Putting Coronavirus on Death Certificates and Urged an End to Shutdowns," *Daily Mail*, updated April 29, 2020, https://www.dailymail.co.uk/news/article-8269475/YouTube-accused-censorship-removing-videos-criticize-shutdowns.html.

Susan Wojcicki, even came out on April 22, 2020, as saying YouTube would delete anything that contradicts the World Health Organization on COVID-19.[22]

In addition, Facebook's Mark Zuckerberg boasted, "The world has faced pandemics before, but this time we have a new superpower: the ability to gather and share data for good."[23] Innocent enough, you might say, but really, he openly admitted that personal data collected by Facebook will be shared with authorities to help save lives in the COVID-19 event. All things are permissible in a medical emergency, it seems.

Civil liberties lost during times of crisis are seldom restored in full when the panic is over. What is so rapidly happening now does not auger well for a return to life as we knew it a few months ago in both America and in the world at large. The new normal may never be like the old normal.

A quick observation about the impact on the US Constitution at this point. Are parts of the US Constitution being shredded before our eyes by a virus? No, seriously. It has been shocking how Americans have rolled over on their constitutionally protected rights as state governors and local

---

22 Martin Bürger, "YouTube CEO: We'll Delete Anything That Contradicts World Health Organization on COVID-19," LifeSite News, April 22, 2020, https://www.lifesitenews.com/news/youtube-ceo-well-delete-anything-that-contradicts-word-health-organization-on-covid-19.

23 Mark Zuckerberg, "How Data Can Aid the Fight against Covid-19," Washington Post, April 20, 2020, https://www.washingtonpost.com/opinions/2020/04/20/how-data-can-aid-fight-against-covid-19/.

authorities have put out mandatory measures, like social/physical distancing, masks, gloves, and lockdowns. People have been arrested for surfing in the ocean and walking alone in the park. Skateboard parks have been filled in with sand to stop youngsters from enjoying some healthy playtime. These measures have been promoted as supposedly saving lives, and anyone who pushes back against them is labeled as dangerously heartless and uncaring.

Studies show that sunlight and fresh air are good for you (sunlight builds vitamin D) and even kills the coronavirus in minutes versus hours compared to when you are all cooped up in small indoor spaces. Yep, it is true.[24]

WHAT ABOUT MASKS?

To wear or not to wear? That is the question!

In hospital operating rooms, surgical masks are worn to protect the patient under the knife from germs from the doctors and nurses in the room. In the COVID-19 event of 2020, the wearing of masks was deemed not necessary; then they suddenly were. The experts changed their minds in a few short weeks but did not offer any conclusive science to back up their assertions. The wearing of masks became compulsory in many settings, including some shopping establishments and venues. People who wore masks

---

24 See Lydia Smith, "Sunlight Kills Coronavirus Quickly, Says Top DHS Official," *Newsweek*, April 24, 2020, https://www.newsweek.com/sunlight-kills-coronavirus-scientist-1500012.

continued to touch their faces after not even washing their hands, rebreathe their own viruses (not a good thing for a healthy person walking around), and reduce their oxygen intake, all of which are not good for maintaining an individual's strong immune system.

Here is a quote from the website of family physician Dr. David Brownstein (West Bloomfield, MI) regarding masks:

> It should be well known that cloth masks, bandanas, or handkerchiefs will do very little to stop the spread of coronavirus. In fact, they may actually increase your risk of becoming ill from corona and other influenza-like illnesses. A 2015 study found cloth masks, when compared to surgical masks, increase the rate of influenza-like illnesses 13x! (1) Cloth masks are probably best avoided and should not be reused without properly sanitizing them.[25]

Masks were used to stop people from coughing and sneezing on others and spreading the virus through the air, and government health officials and even members of the public began to shame those who did not wear masks as people who did not "care about lives."

All the while, officials allowed "essential services"—like liquor stores, marijuana outlets, and Planned Parenthood

---

25 Dr. David Brownstein, "We Must Wear Face Masks? Show Me the Science Behind That!," LewRockwell.com, April 28, 2020, https://www.lewrockwell.com/2020/04/dr-david-brownstein/we-must-wear-face-masks-show-me-the-science-behind-that/.

abortion mills—to stay open. Perhaps continued tax revenue from these enterprises was a big factor here.

The different types of masks deliver differing results. Homemade fabric masks are the least effective in preventing someone from breathing in the virus and becoming infected, while N95 masks, properly fitted, are more protective. However, these are not readily available to the public. Masks do seem to help in stopping much of what gets projected out when coughing and sneezing. To date no conclusive scientific studies have been made to ascertain whether wearing masks is effective. Scientists are still debating whether the flu viruses are spread by aerosol effect (through the air).

Some doctors have argued that wearing gloves is more effective than wearing masks, as the coronavirus 2 stays active on surfaces longer than the SARS 1 and MERS viruses did.

Notably, fresh air, sunshine, exercise, good wholesome non-GMO food, necessary supplements, a positive outlook on life—all play a role in promoting health by strengthening the immune system. Masks do not outweigh these for the non-health-compromised population. Certainly, the wearing of masks in targeted demographics, like the elderly in nursing homes and the immune compromised, is warranted, but to expect everyone to wear masks all the time out in public is not. A "one size fits all" approach is not the way to go.

Of course, hindsight is always 20/20, but among the laymen I talked to as this pandemic began to break in February and March 2020, the consensus was that the authorities were "spooked," to use common parlance. All that fancy modeling that predicted up to two million Americans dying from COVID-19 seemed, at that time, to be out in left field. Perhaps this is too harsh an assessment, but hopefully history will tell whether an *agenda* was hiding in plain sight. Specific targeting of any mitigation efforts rather than widespread saturation might well be the watchword of the future.

HERD IMMUNITY

Herd immunity develops when the infection rate in a population reaches over 60 to 70 percent. The virus has fewer and fewer high-risk people to attack in this scenario and soon peters out (fewer people are now part of the chain of infection being passed on). This has been the experience of past pandemics. Most people who go through a viral event or season do not die, and data shows that so far with COVID-19, many people do not even experience any serious symptoms.

Of course, COVID-19 is a new or "novel" strain of coronavirus and may require a slightly higher herd immunity infection rate of over 70 percent. COVID-19 appears to be more contagious than other, earlier coronaviruses, but in light of antibody test surveys coming out, not more deadly. The mindset that we must do something drastic to "stop the virus" is simply not accurate. The way the virus is stopped is to attain herd immunity. If you artificially tamper with the process, you may "flatten the curve" and thus avoid overloading the health-care system for a while, but you still do not stop the virus altogether.[26]

Then, some theorists have gone so far as to suggest that the newness and infectiousness of COVID-19 may well have been "engineered," and not the result of some curious animal-to-human transmission story from a wet market in Wuhan. Time will tell whether such a theory holds water. Consider the source and context of the outbreak. Close to the wet market in Wuhan, China, there is a biological weapons lab. This year, 2020, is an election year with a trade war going on between China and the US. Trump's goal has been to make America great again, and that means (among other things) taking on the huge deficits in trade with China through the new deal he made. China does not like the pushback and remains committed to its worldwide empire-building agenda. The globalists' agenda is also advanced by a weakened American economy (because of the medical lockdowns), a situation that favors China and hits at the heart of Trump's campaign promise to "make America great again."

Too far out? The stuff of conspiracy? Truth is sometimes stranger than fiction, they say. Stop, drop the rocks, and think about it.

The COVID-19 event is still unfolding at a rapid pace as of this writing, but it has seen what appears to be a huge

---

26 See Sam Meredith, "HEALTH AND SCIENCE, Flattening the Coronavirus Curve: What This Means and Why It Matters," CNBC, March 19, 2020, https://www.cnbc.com/2020/03/19/coronavirus-what-does-flattening-the-curve-mean-and-why-it-matters.html.

lurch toward central government control in the day-to-day affairs of Joe Citizen. All levels of society, local and national, have been impacted by this event. It could be argued that a nationally coordinated response to the invisible enemy was logical and needed to oversee efforts to curb the pandemic.

However, such measures as contact tracing (soon to be rolled out in many places through smartphone technology at least) will mean that your every move and contact can potentially be tracked—all in the name of a medical emergency. We have already been told that another wave of the pandemic is likely on its way, and so on each year. This could mean that such measures could indeed become part of the new normal. The authorities would have cover for using the data collected for medical purposes in other ways. They already do in China in the creation of individual citizen "social scores," where you are rewarded for behaving the way the authorities want you to behave or penalized for perceived misbehavior.

SPECIAL EDITORIAL NOTE

As the spring of 2020 advanced, and temperatures rose, people wanted to get out and about and soak up some sunshine, at least here in Washington State. They also wanted to get back to work—those who still had jobs. People began to question the numbers put out by the authorities, and momentum built to start pushing back on government overreach. It seemed as if the people were not as scared as before. Protests were starting all over the country, and business owners even risked their licenses by opening against state directives.

While President Trump was clearly encouraging the states to start opening up in phases, the medical hard-liners were crying, "Watch out! If we move too fast, we will run into trouble," and so it went until at least mid-June 2020, when this book went to the publisher.

10

CLIMATE CHANGE

THINGS ARE HOTTING UP

> *"While the earth remains, seedtime and harvest, cold and heat, winter and summer, and day and night shall not cease."*
>
> —GENESIS 8:22

Climate change advocates have had a lot to say this century about the dire consequences of not controlling "global warming," as it used to be called. Somewhat humorously, real scientific data (and not just modeling) has shown a cooling trend in the last twenty years. Of course, temperatures have been rising since the last "mini ice age" that we began to come out of in the mid-1800s. The problem is measuring any temperature increase over a long time and separating out the human impact of burning fossil fuels, for example, in a modern economy. It is right here that data gives way to ideology, and political agendas mixed in with environmentalism drive policy.

Climate change alarmists say we must make radical changes now; otherwise the ocean levels will rise, flooding coastal cities; more and more devastating fires will break out; famines and catastrophic weather will occur; and large-scale civil and national unrest will follow. They argue that rising levels of greenhouse gases are a problem (more specifically, carbon dioxide, which is a naturally occurring gas vital to plant life and all human existence). Pollution is at unacceptable levels and comes mostly from fossil fuels (coal, petroleum, and natural gas), which must be dramatically lowered worldwide if we as a planet are to avoid catastrophe within a few short years.

According to the "Green New Deal" advocates in the radical socialist wing of the Democratic Party, we only have approximately twelve years to go.[1] Remember Paul Ehrlich and the *Population Bomb* scare tactic he employed in the 1970s saying the planet had only fifteen years or so to go before disastrous consequences unfolded if we did not drastically reduce the earth's population?

---

[1] See William Cummings, "'The World Is Going to End in 12 Years If We Don't Address Climate Change,' Ocasio-Cortez Says," *USA Today*, January 22, 2019, https://www.usatoday.com/story/news/politics/onpolitics/2019/01/22/ocasio-cortez-climate-change-alarm/2642481002/.

CLIMATE CHANGE

Climate change advocates seem to agree that America should lead the way in reducing carbon emissions, while China and India (the greatest polluters in the world) get a pass for now. A form of "carbon tax" will fund projects to mitigate the causes of so-called planetary climate change.

As it turns out, America does lead the way in carbon emission reduction worldwide, and voluntarily so. Pushback (Trump withdrawing America from the Paris climate accord) has slowed the rush toward world centralized control of individual nation states as it pertains to their economies and "responsibilities" toward the planet. We are told that "we are in this together," and scientific/political elites should tell us what is needed. Problem is, there appears to be an underlying agenda: a socialist world government New World Order that advocates more solutions, regulation, taxation, and redistribution of wealth as nations enjoy less and less national sovereignty.

The IPCC, or Intergovernmental Panel on Climate Change, established in 1988, is now an arm of the United Nations, dedicated to providing the world with objective, scientific information in order to understand the risk of human-induced climate change, and its natural, economic, and sociopolitical impacts and risks. The IPCC is to posit responses and action to be taken to offset damaging climate change. Of course, climate and weather patterns do cross political borders, so international cooperation in this matter is required. But to what degree and based on what science becomes important.

It is naive to think that secular progressive humanists

in this organization always know best for everyone. Then, when it comes to Hollywood celebrities and the likes of Al Gore jetting around the globe in their gas-guzzling private jets, we see that hypocrisy is no place to start. Why not catch a sailboat to the next climate change conference you attend instead of expanding your global "carbon footprint"?

Climate change science is *not* "settled," despite the ridicule heaped on those who disagree by politicians and global ideologues.[2] Meteorological and climatic dynamics are so complex that no definitive assertions about "human"-induced climate change can honestly be made. The emphasis here is on honesty. When you take the time to look at contrasting science, you have to conclude that science *does not show* that human influence alone is the driving factor for temperature rises over the last 170 years.

Consider climate modeling and projections. These are based on assumptions that often reflect agenda-based research, where the desired result skews the interpretation of the data. So-called science guys are trotted out to tout the narrative, and seemingly little clear-thinking debate is allowed in the public domain. Name-calling occurs often, as climate change "deniers" are ridiculed and sidelined to silence their different conclusions and opinions. *Hot*heads seem to prevail over cooler ones.

---

2   See, for example, Jeffrey Kluger, "How Climate Deniers Try to Sow Confusion," Time, April 28, 2016, https://time.com/4308518/climate-change-settled-science/.

CLIMATE CHANGE

Solar intensity fluctuations, worldwide ocean dynamics, even incomplete and suspect land-derived weather and climate data (weather stations are not consistently placed in areas that are uniformly distant from local influencing factors, such as buildings and urban heat islands)—these inconsistencies throw doubt on the drastic climate predictions of many environmentalist policy makers.

World climate change advocates argue that far-reaching legislative and policy measures in land, energy, industry, social, geographic, and transport sectors should be overseen by the United Nations, a globalist entity. Mankind should be eating less meat; riding bicycles; using mass transit, like buses, light rail, and trains; living in smaller houses or apartments; and switching to renewable energy sources, such as wind, solar, tidal, and hydroelectric power. In this way the planet will be more sustainable, especially if we can slow and reduce population growth.

The United Nations Agenda 2030 Goal #10 aims to reduce inequality among nations through wealth redistribution: classic socialism, which some progressive leftists with heart would have you believe is simply "fair, and the right thing to do." To achieve this goal, they advocate fundamental changes in the way societies produce and consume goods and services. These changes and control can only be achieved through strong centralized government planning and oversight.

The environmentalist movement today operates within this socialist/communist context where in effect individual liberty must be curtailed. Insiders admit this. In the United States, environmental groups such as the Sierra Club and the Cousteau Society historically have not only worked toward cleaner air and water, things we all enjoy and aspire to in all parts of the world, but have also lobbied for a variety of leftist causes, like abortion, unilateral disarmament, and labor union practices, to name a few. Some have even called these groups "watermelons": green on the outside but pink on the inside, where socialism has been dressed up in environmental terms. Back in 1990 Mikhail Gorbachev, a globalist, called for a worldwide green organization to unlock a new world order. His plan included influencing gullible dupes in academia, the sciences, the press, and yes, politicians too, like Al Gore, with scary environmental stories.

In the modern oil war of the 2010s and beyond, Russian green types along with US green types share the goal of crippling US oil production through anti-fracking and by blocking oil pipeline initiatives. This happened during the Obama administration, but of course, things have changed since an administration change in 2016 under Donald Trump.

Climate change hysteria is not really about the environment, or saving the planet, even. We all agree that a greener planet is better than a parched brown one. So why is it that Greens are not rejoicing over the fact that according to the journal *Nature Climate Change*, over the past few decades, the earth has actually become noticeably greener in areas approximating twice the size of mainland USA? This is a good thing. This global greening has been caused primarily by the increased concentration of CO_2 in the earth's atmosphere. Remember: CO_2 is essential to green plant growth, so much so that greenhouse plant growers routinely pump in huge proportions of CO_2 to promote growth in their greenhouses. Even Green New Deal advocates have certainly enjoyed eating the luscious produce from such farming operations. Some of them may even smoke some of the products.

Global climate change advocates promote policies that really are, in the end, bad for poor people, who would benefit more and more from higher CO_2 levels. This despite alarmist cries of how dangerous this naturally occurring so-called pollutant is. Once again, science has not proven that human influence in the twentieth century has definitively caused global warming/climate change. Many reputable climate scientists do not conclude that warming is due mostly to man's influence.

The so-called 97 percent scientific consensus figure often touted by political and environmental leaders to hammer home the need for severe policies to mitigate man-induced climate change was arrived at by statistically surveying papers written by 928 scientists, not the actual data, methodologies, and conclusions themselves, which are still under debate as research into climate change goes on. In 2004, Naomi Oreskes surveyed 928 peer-reviewed climate papers published between 1993 and 2003, finding none that rejected the human cause of global warming. Please note that the content of papers was not reviewed, simply a statistical analysis of how many papers dealt with the subject of global warming and the supposed human causes.

Apparently, we have here a tyranny of the majority, where because the majority think one way, the rest must think the same way. In the past those who thought the earth was flat or that it was at the center of the solar system were in the majority. Those who thought otherwise were demonized till scientific truth eventually broke the stranglehold.

Groupthink shuts down free and fair research and debate, a hallmark of scientific discovery, and it has intimidated many scientists into keeping quiet for fear of losing their jobs at universities largely controlled by progressive leftists with an agenda.

So, what about alternative energy sources, like wind and solar, producing enough electricity for all the new wave battery-driven bicycles and cars, buses, and trucks, industry, manufacturing, and household/business needs? Can they consistently and cheaply deliver energy to fuel our modern economies?

These sources have proven problematic in that they are not as reliable as fossil fuel and certainly nuclear power generation of electricity. In fact, electric cars depend mostly (over 50 percent when averaged out globally) on fossil fuel and nuclear-generated electricity, especially when the wind is not blowing and the sun is not shining intensely enough. Then, the carnage of birds killed by wind turbine propellers, turbine fires, and waste disposal problems of these huge rigs are only some of the additional problems faced with this energy source. Who wants to look at hundreds of square miles of windmills or solar modules?

Advocates of nuclear power argue that it is historically and statistically the safest form of power generation, despite the well-publicized Chernobyl incident in Russia and the Fukushima incident in Japan. France leads the way by percentage with 71.7 percent of its electricity produced by nuclear power. Slovakia follows with 55 percent, and the US is way down the world's top fifteen list, at the bottom, with 19.3 percent.[3] We have a huge abundance of fossil fuel resources to generate electricity with, and with more effort can do so more cleanly.

To start reducing dependence on fossil fuels to zero in ten years as suggested by Representative Alexandria Ocasio-Cortez is grossly impractical. There is no way you can ramp up alternative energy sources to 100 percent in such a short time, even if you wanted to.

WEATHER AND CLIMATE ALTERATION

Weather- and climate-altering proposals have been made by the likes of none other than Bill Gates. He has been funding the Stratospheric Controlled Perturbation Experiment (SCoPEx) at Harvard, which hopes to sprinkle chalk dust at high stratospheric levels to shade the earth from the sun's rays with a view to slowing the atmospheric heating trend. The

---

3   See Wikipedia, s.v. "nuclear power by country," accessed June 18, 2020, https://en.wikipedia.org/wiki/Nuclear_power_by_country.

test would be local, but there is concern that the weather and climatic processes are so complex and interconnected worldwide that the experiment could prove dangerous.

The project is now on hold, having been inspired in part by huge volcanic eruptions: Mount Pinatubo in the Philippines in 1991 and Mount Tambora, Indonesia, in 1815. The latter affected weather patterns around the world according to records in America, Ireland, and Switzerland, which pointed to what was called "the Year Without a Summer."[4] The planet cooled for a short period due to these two volcanic eruptions.

Could this climate-altering project on a global scale, if ever implemented, be about population control through what some call environmental geoengineering?

Incidentally, Operation Popeye was a military-based cloud seeding program during the Vietnam War that systematically affected the weather in Vietnam, Laos, and Cambodia. The goal was to bog down the enemy Vietcong supply lines through the effects of excessive rain. US planes dropped dry ice particles in the fog and clouds to increase precipitation and bog down the mostly dirt roads used by the Vietcong. This covert program occurred under the Johnson administration, and guided by Henry Kissinger, seemed to have done the trick. There was indeed abnormal

---

4   See Evan Andrews, "What Was the "Year Without a Summer"?," History, updated August 22, 2018, https://www.history.com/news/what-was-the-year-without-a-summer.

precipitation, and the severe flooding of Vietnam in 1971 was attributed to the cloud seeding. However, when the public found out in 1972, the operation abruptly stopped.

GEORGE SOROS'S INFLUENCE IN GLOBAL MATTERS THROUGH HIS OPEN SOCIETY NETWORK

To be fair, besides Bill Gates's involvement in world population and climate matters, the other key "philanthropic" activist, billionaire George Soros, has been playing a significant role in promoting global goals.

Soros, born a Hungarian to a wealthy Jewish family, escaped the Holocaust by posing as a Christian godson of an official whose role it was to confiscate goods taken from Jews being shipped off to Nazi work and death camps. At age fourteen, he helped this official perform his duties for the Nazis, and later Soros explained his rationale in a *60 Minutes* interview done in 1998, claiming that he really was only a spectator, and that if he had not done it, someone else would have.

Recently, Hungary, which has enjoyed a populist pushback against Socialist globalist trends in their country and Europe as a whole, has seen George Soros as a "serious threat to national security."[5] His efforts in aiding illegal immigrants from the Syrian conflict were seen to be part of

---

5   About Hungary, "George Soros and His Network Pose a Serious Threat to Hungary's National Security," *News in Brief,* September 25, 2017, http://abouthungary.hu/news-in-brief/george-soros-and-his-network-pose-a-serious-threat-to-hungarys-national-security/.

destabilizing Hungary. Soros, and a university he funded there, have been run out of Hungary.

Soros has funded his Open Society Network with more than $8 billion to "support individuals and organizations [in more than 120 countries] across the globe fighting for freedom of expression, accountable government, and societies that promote justice and equality."[6] This all sounds wonderful, except that George Soros supports leftist/socialist causes that advocate everything from open borders, voter registration, and media research groups (like Media Matters), to women's rights and groups that support abortion.

Along with Bill Gates and others, Soros has supported the recent climate change activism by standing behind young Greta Thunberg, the daughter of famous opera singer and left-liberal activist Malena Ernman. Greta's "handlers" are seasoned activists such as German Luisa-Marie Neubauer, who, through groups like ONE (which fights against global extreme poverty, hunger, and preventable disease), use her as the young face of a concerned generation fearful of the future if we don't do something drastic right now about climate change. Does it concern you that Greta's Asperger's form of autism may be exploited by these handlers?

---

6   "George Soros: Founder/Chair," Open Society Foundations website, accessed June 11, 2020, https://www.opensocietyfoundations.org/george-soros.

POPULATION CONTROL, CLIMATE CONTROL, AND ENVIRONMENTALISM

In summary, the "new" socialism, which has gained momentum in the two decades of the twenty-first century, is so intertwined with environmentalism (population and climate control) as to be indistinguishable.

How convenient to be hidden in plain sight.

11

WHAT IS THE AGENDA BEHIND THE AGENDA?

GREEN IS THE NEW RED

And God saw that it was good.

—GENESIS 1:12

Globalists argue that global problems require global solutions. Vehicles like the United Nations and all its subsidiaries are ideal in advancing their agendas. We now investigate the following two significant agenda programs.

AGENDA

AGENDA 21 (AND ITS LATEST VERSION, AGENDA 2030)

They have an agenda. But who are "they"?

They are people of influence (academically, politically, financially, socially, and administratively) who share a similar worldview. Can you make a definitive list of these people? Yes and no. You must step back and connect the dots between what is really going on in the web of human experience, who the leaders are, where the money is flowing from, and to what purpose.

Put another way, what is the agenda behind the agenda, and what has this to do with socialism and a New World Order?

Let us begin with the United Nations' own information from its website regarding Agenda 21, and then its latest version, Agenda 2030.

Agenda 21 was agreed upon by 178 member countries of the United Nations at a conference in Rio de Janeiro in 1992. It was based on the UN's "sustainability" goals, and more recently has been encompassed by Agenda 2030. This latest outline goes way beyond the largely environmental goals of Agenda 21 to include a wide-ranging set of measures to radically transform all societies everywhere. Global governance is the key here.

Look up Agenda 2030 on the internet and see how the comprehensive goals are all presented. It was adopted in 2015 at the United Nations 70th General Assembly by 193 member nations, to thunderous applause. Top socialist former NATO chief Javier Solana celebrated the plan, which was approved at the summit as the next "Great Leap Forward"—the old campaign slogan of the Chinese Communist Party under Chairman Mao (in China, where an estimated forty-five million Chinese were worked, starved, or beaten to death in the late 1950s and early '60s).

The UN plan to transform the world would leave no one behind, with everyone involved. The preamble reads, "All countries and all stakeholders, acting in collaborative partnership, will implement this plan."[1]

The planet is described as "Mother Earth" and will be healed in this process.[2] Humanity will be freed from the tyranny of poverty with the future of the humanity and the planet lying in "our hands."[3]

It is a universal plan: a "charter for people and planet in the twenty-first century."[4]

Notably, God and His plan for man and the planet are ignored. It is not "Father God" but "Mother Earth"!

---

1 "Transforming Our World: The 2030 Agenda for Sustainable Development," Sustainable Development Goals Knowledge Platform, accessed June 11, 2020, https://sustainabledevelopment.un.org/post2015/transformingourworld, preamble.

2 "Transforming Our World," par. 59 under "Sustainable Development Goals and targets."

3 "Transforming Our World," par. 53 under "A call for action to change our world."

4 "Transforming Our World," par. 51 under "A call for action to change our world."

AGENDA

A striking feature of Agenda 2030 is a road map to global socialism and corporatism where governments and individuals are called upon to reduce inequality by sharing wealth and by addressing income inequality. Governments must seize control of the means of production, either directly or indirectly, and make fundamental changes in the way societies produce and consume goods and services. Current lifestyles of the affluent middle class must be altered to consume less, and thus make sustainability possible. Western aid (redistribution of wealth) should flow to poorer nations, including those ruled by socialist/totalitarian regimes, who conveniently will take care of their people.

Universal health coverage is another goal. This includes vaccines for all, and sexual and reproductive health care services for all—code for abortion and contraception. National strategies and programs are to ensure these goals are met. Obamacare fitted in quite well here.

Sustainable cities and communities are to be achieved by concentrating populations in urban areas, where private property ownership is largely restricted, and many of the new generation is to be stacked and packed in mid- and high-rises. Walking and riding bikes, reducing single car travel, and utilizing mass transit are to be encouraged in this urban utopia by means of town planning initiatives and policies, paid for by tax dollars.

Do they really want to cram and control all people into narrow urban areas and corridors so that animals can have more room to roam and make everything more

WHAT IS THE AGENDA BEHIND THE AGENDA?

"sustainable"? I live in the Seattle area, and have seen what that looks like with the implementation of a policy of "stack 'em and pack 'em." Mid-rise apartment blocks have become the norm in places like Redmond, Kirkland, Bothell, and Kenmore in the greater Seattle metro.

Information flow (aka propaganda) will ensure that the next generation will all be "agents of change."[5] The UN explicitly defines this aspect in the agreement as follows:

> By 2030, ensure that all learners acquire the knowledge and skills needed to promote sustainable development, including, among others, through education for sustainable development and sustainable lifestyles, human rights, gender equality, promotion of a culture of peace and non-violence, global citizenship and appreciation of cultural diversity and of culture's contribution to sustainable development.[6]

Education, education, education, or as some would say, programming to adopt population control, central planning, and global governance while riding on the back of a youthful desire for a "better world."[7] Older people want a better world too, by the way; it just appears that younger people have more passion. Perhaps they are not so tired, yet.

---

5   "Transforming Our World," par. 51.

6   "Transforming Our World," goal 4: 4.7.

7   "Transforming Our World," par. 51 under "A call for action to change our world."

AGENDA

The project would cost trillions of dollars per year and be financed through a variety of means public and private, not to exclude such devices as a worldwide "carbon tax."

Agenda 2030 was lauded by socialist and Islamic dictators alike, including since-deceased Robert Mugabe of Zimbabwe, whose African-style socialism utterly impoverished a once-thriving economy. Communist China, known for its religious and political persecution, censorship, and forced abortions in its one-child policy, also boasted of playing a crucial role in crafting Agenda 2030. Leftists in Western countries and leaders in the European Union are on board with this agenda too.

Pope Francis of the Catholic Church got involved by addressing the UN with a plea to support the UN goals of Agenda 2030. This pope is considered by many to fall into the "social justice"/socialist side of political persuasion. He leans toward aspects of liberation theology.

On the surface some of the Sustainable Development Goals (SDGs) of Agenda 2030 seem quite reasonable: clean air, water, education, eradication of poverty, protection of life below water and on land, affordable and clean energy for all, climate change mitigation measures, and so on. Who can argue that the world does not need or desire these?

Well, some do, pointing to controversial elements like climate change and gender issues. They argue that the socialist-driven road map (or means to these ends) is faulty if not dangerous to long-held Western values and practices. Wealth redistribution, centralized control of the means of production and their distribution, and central governance, with its myriad of laws and regulations, are elements that spell *AGENDA*.

Of course, capitalism has been systematically vilified as "evil" and "exploitative," and a concerted effort has been made to target the US as the chief world villain in this. "Structural" or "systemic" change is needed in the US and the world, so the argument goes. Yet it is my conviction that when you leave out fallen human nature, with its selfish tendencies (and God's help through Jesus' saving grace), you will not be able to successfully achieve any laudable and sustainable goals.

Personal repentance, rebirth, renewal, and reformation follow in that order. Change happens from the inside out. True transformation and a love for your fellow man starts with a work of grace in your heart, where you learn to love God first. It is about relationship, not rules and regulations.

> I will give you a new heart and put a new spirit within you; I will take the heart of stone out of your flesh and give you a heart of flesh. I will put My Spirit within you and cause you to walk in My statutes, and you will keep My judgments and do them. Then you shall dwell in the land that I gave to your fathers; you shall be My people, and I will be your God. I will deliver you from all your uncleannesses. I will call for the grain and multiply it, and bring no famine upon you. And I will multiply the fruit of your trees and the increase of your fields, so that you need never again bear the reproach of famine among the nations.
>
> —EZEKIEL 36:26-30

12

WAS JESUS A SOCIALIST?

THE TRUE AND THE FALSE GOSPEL

> *The Spirit of the L*ORD *is upon Me,*
> *Because He has anointed Me*
> *To preach the gospel to the poor;*
> *He has sent Me to heal the brokenhearted,*
> *To proclaim liberty to the captives*
> *And recovery of sight to the blind,*
> *To set at liberty those who are oppressed;*
> *To proclaim the acceptable year of the L*ORD*."*
>
> —LUKE 4:18-19

Politicians sometimes use Jesus for their own political ends and often mess up with the context and meaning of scripture passages they use to make their points.

For starters, Jesus never called for central planning of the economy by so-called elites; neither did he call for the radical distribution of wealth. Jesus was not a "communist" living in a collective commune, although He did share quality time and live in close contact with His disciples for a season of intense training. His "liberation" theology had nothing to do with modern liberation theology. His mission was "to seek and to save" the lost from sin and its consequences (Luke 19:10), and He worked on their heart attitudes from the inside out. He knew that if He could turn the hearts of men toward the true and pure God, they would then begin to bear fruits of that righteousness in their dealings with their fellow man. Justice would then prevail.

THE TRUE GOSPEL OF GRACE VERSUS THE FALSE GOSPEL OF LIBERATION THEOLOGY

"Liberation theology" has developed out of an interpretation of what the Bible teaches about the gospel, or good news of man's emancipation from sin. The central mission of the church must address the plight of the poor. True disciples should work toward a just society by encouraging social and political change, especially as it affects the poor. The marginalized poor and downtrodden, whose "rights" are trampled by the "greedy rich," are to be defended in their vulnerability, and doctrine to support this assertion is promoted.

This is not to say that the Bible has nothing to say about believers' responsibility toward the poor. It does, especially in the Old Testament. Several passages, too long to quote here, speak to this, including Leviticus 19:10; Deuteronomy 15:10–11; Proverbs 19:17; Isaiah 58; Amos 5–6; and Zechariah 7:10.

God has always had a heart for suffering people and has called His own followers to play their part in alleviating pain and hopelessness among the poor, not only practically, but also by proclaiming the gospel. When anyone, and this includes the poor, puts their trust in God through Jesus, they will have a very present help in their troubles. Indeed, God will even give them a way of escape out of poverty as they follow His wise direction, freedom, and the possibilities found in a relationship with Christ.

Some liberation theologians use Jesus' words as recorded in Matthew 10:34 to promote social activism in the church. This activism (social unrest and change) was supposedly pushed by Jesus, they say, when He said, "Do not suppose that I have come to bring peace to the earth. I did not come to bring peace, but a sword" (NIV).

I understand this passage to be speaking not of revolutionary societal change but, in context, of a dividing of the lines between those who would and would not forsake all to follow Jesus, including putting love for family members above their love for Him. We know that Jesus supported the family, but any of His followers had to learn from Him before they could genuinely love their families.

AGENDA

Liberation theology had its roots and significant growth in Latin America in Roman Catholicism (whose followers have always been big on good works, which of course are not bad in themselves). The widespread poverty and mistreatment of the poor have been common in many countries in Latin America, so liberation theology found fertile ground. Many countries in South America are now experiencing significant outpourings of the Holy Spirit in mass meetings taking place in stadiums across the continent. The Catholic Church's grip on South America has weakened, to the consternation of many in the Vatican, as the Protestant movements have grown in influence.

Liberation theology is often associated with Marxism and seen as a religious form of socialist policies where the core tenets of the historical Christian faith (grace, faith, repentance, and trust in Christ alone for the forgiveness of sin) are of lesser importance than activism toward helping the poor. Mankind's primary need remains spiritual at its core, not social, with its societal systems. Corrupt social systems spring from the corrupt hearts and minds of people, not systems.

Jesus thus goes after the hearts of needy people through love, compassion, service, and sacrifice. God loves both the rich and the poor and seeks to bring unity (and fairness) around His example: His life and death on the cross.

Liberation theology has also taken root outside of Latin America in places like Cuba and South Africa, where I saw firsthand the injustices of the apartheid era. These injustices have been addressed through significant government top-down intervention, with mixed results. Churches in South Africa led much of the charge against injustice toward the poor, playing a leading role in working against racism. Nobel Peace Prize winner Desmond Tutu, a cleric, campaigned against apartheid all his life, adopting what many call a liberation theological approach to the gospel. Many other clerics, however, concentrated on preaching a gospel that began with heart transformation, which later translated into helping the poor thereafter.

To dig a bit deeper, we will investigate several scriptures from the Bible that focus on how Jesus handled various life challenges, which have been used to support the notion that Jesus was a socialist.

A WEALTH DISTRIBUTION ISSUE

In the first of these passages, Jesus was confronted by an envious man upset about the culture's custom of distributing the family inheritance or wealth. He wanted Jesus to intervene in his cause.

> Then one from the crowd said to Him, "Teacher, tell my brother to divide the inheritance with me."
> But He said to him, "Man, who made Me a judge or an arbitrator over you?" And He said to them, "Take heed and beware of covetousness, for one's life does not consist in the abundance of the things he possesses." (Luke 12:13–14)

Jesus rebuked the challenger for being presumptuous about His role as arbiter in such matters, and zeroed in on the man's covetousness, pointing out that life does not consist in one's wealth. He was not going to be drawn into the squabble about the "inequalities" of the family inheritance rules of the day; rather, he focused on the man's heart need, which was far more important than trying to get his "fair share."

THE PARABLE OF THE TALENTS

In the parable of the talents, recorded in Matthew 25:14–30, Jesus praised those stewards who profited with what was given them but rebuked the unprofitable servant, who fearfully hid his talent till the master's return. It seems as if God (Jesus) has no problem with trading and making a profit. Was He a socialist? I think not. Read the passage for yourself. Throughout the Bible God is not opposed to making a profit.

THE DIFFICULTY OF THE RICH ENTERING HEAVEN

Jesus did actually speak of the difficulty of a rich man entering the kingdom of heaven. Matthew 19:23 tells us:

> Then Jesus said to His disciples, "Assuredly, I say to you that it is hard for a rich man to enter the kingdom of heaven."

At first glance it appears as if Jesus is against the rich. However, the issue here is not the amount of money itself; it is the love of it that is a concern. The heart matter of trust that an individual puts in money rather than in God is the focus. The rich young ruler, who approached Jesus earlier in the chapter, was reluctant to part with His wealth. He was even proud because he was able to meet all of God's standards in the Jewish law of Moses, or so he thought. Jesus had to expose the fact that the young man's love of money was getting in the way of his relationship with Jesus. He did so by telling him to give his wealth away.

You only find out what sort of hold something has on you when you are asked to give it up. You do not really know what is in your heart until that point.

I have a suspicion that many of the folk who want you to give up your wealth by consenting to higher taxes for the rich are not willing to give up theirs. They are happy to redistribute your wealth, especially if they are happily and largely employed by the governments that do the distributions.

THE CLEANSING OF THE TEMPLE

When Jesus kicked out the money changers from the temple precincts in Jerusalem, was He promoting socialism by confronting gross greed and profiteering, or was it something else going on here?

> Then Jesus went into the temple of God and drove out all those who bought and sold in the temple, and overturned the tables of the money changers and the seats of those who sold doves. And He said to them, "It is written, 'My house shall be called a house of prayer,' but you have made it a 'den of thieves.'" (Matthew 21:12–13)

His primary concern was for the purity of the temple's purpose—a place to meet with God in prayer. Pure temple worship had been corrupted, and God's house needed a cleanup. We have no record of Jesus overturning the tables in the local marketplace. Greed and usury have no place in God's economy, wherever it's found, but to use this incident to allude to Jesus' "socialistic" tendencies is a bit of a stretch.

HELPING THE NEEDY

Piecing together not only the words of Jesus Himself but those of His prophets and apostles, we see that God's will is for His people to reflect in practical terms His heart toward the poor, and indeed others in need, such as vulnerable widows and orphans. Of course, in our society today, there are agencies that cover areas where local church groups do not, but as a whole, the responsibility of the church is not to abdicate its role in this to the government but to fulfill its responsibilities.

Look at these Bible injunctions to reach out to the needy:

> "For the poor will never cease from the land; therefore I command you, saying, 'You shall open your hand wide to your brother, to your poor and your needy, in your land.'" (Deuteronomy 15:11)

> Pure and undefiled religion before God and the Father is this: to visit orphans and widows in their trouble, and to keep oneself unspotted from the world. (James 1:27)

But whoever has this world's goods, and sees his brother in need, and shuts up his heart from him, how does the love of God abide in him?

My little children, let us not love in word or in tongue, but in deed and in truth. (1 John 3:17–18)

Jesus, speaking through the apostle John, is opposed to hypocrisy. The church is called to make a practical difference in helping the poor and indeed does so all around the world, especially if you take an honest, unjaundiced look at the matter.

Having said all this, it is important to point out that the poor still need the gospel proclaimed to them, as it is the good news of Jesus coming to help mankind in its deepest heart need that lays a foundation for any lasting change in a poor person's life. Preaching good news of God's care for the needy is not all so much hot air.

"The Spirit of the LORD is upon Me,
  Because He has anointed Me
  To preach the gospel to the poor. (Luke 4:18)

That same Spirit or anointing is upon His people today to make a difference in poor people's lives. Personal discipleship where the needy are taught and encouraged to follow Jesus' ways of faith and obedience is God's means toward the end of enjoying the freedom of a saving relationship with God through Jesus.

AGENDA

THE GOOD SAMARITAN STORY

In this story the traveler, a Samaritan—an outcast in Jewish society and despised by the religious Jews of the day—takes immediate and personal action to help a man beaten up by the side of the road. No questions were even asked about whether the man deserved help. The Samaritan simply stepped in and used his personal resources to alleviate the man's suffering. He was this man's safety net when trouble hit. He did not hand the man over to the local social worker and sign him up on a welfare program. You get the picture.

> Then Jesus answered and said: "A certain man went down from Jerusalem to Jericho, and fell among thieves, who stripped him of his clothing, wounded him, and departed, leaving him half dead. Now by chance a certain priest came down that road. And when he saw him, he passed by on the other side. Likewise a Levite, when he arrived at the place, came and looked, and passed by on the other side. But a certain Samaritan, as he journeyed, came where he was. And when he saw him, he had compassion. So he went to him and bandaged his wounds, pouring on oil and wine; and he set him on his own animal, brought him to an inn, and took care of him. (Luke 10:30–34)

Jesus contrasted the Samaritan's compassion with the coldness of the priest and the Levite, who ought to have obeyed the word they most certainly knew from the Law.

"RENDER TO CAESAR WHAT IS CAESAR'S"

When Jesus was challenged about taxes in an effort to trap Him and embarrass Him, He outsmarted His detractors by drawing a distinction between two kingdoms: that of Rome (on Earth) and that of God (in heaven). The Jews of the day smarted under repressive Roman rule and wanted to throw the Romans off by political revolution. They expected the Messiah to lead them in this, just as Moses in days of old led God's people out from under the Egyptian Pharaoh's control.

Jesus remained steadfast to His mission: to change the hearts of men, not to get sidetracked into a tax issue. "Give to Caesar his stupid taxes," He might have said in our language, but be sure to give God what belongs to Him: your life, love, worship, and service.

> And Jesus answered and said to them, "Render to Caesar the things that are Caesar's, and to God the things that are God's." And they marveled at Him. (Mark 12:17)

There are literally millions of believers who pay taxes and give freely of their substance to advance God's kingdom on earth through the church and allied ministry endeavors. We can navigate the imperfections of life—even an unfavorable government, with its taxation and regulations—with God's help and wisdom.

AGENDA

THE PARABLE OF THE WORKERS IN THE VINEYARD (PRINCIPLE OF SUPPLY AND DEMAND?)

"For the kingdom of heaven is like a landowner who went out early in the morning to hire laborers for his vineyard. Now when he had agreed with the laborers for a denarius a day, he sent them into his vineyard. And he went out about the third hour and saw others standing idle in the marketplace, and said to them, 'You also go into the vineyard, and whatever is right I will give you.' So they went. Again he went out about the sixth and the ninth hour, and did likewise. And about the eleventh hour he went out and found others standing idle, and said to them, 'Why have you been standing here idle all day?' They said to him, 'Because no one hired us.' He said to them, 'You also go into the vineyard, and whatever is right you will receive.'" (Matthew 20:1–7)

As you can see, the landowner in this story hired laborers at the beginning of the day, and then throughout the day even more.

But to continue the story, when wages were handed out at the end of day, all the hired got the same pay. The laborers hired first complained that the others had gotten the same wages: it was not "fair," as the early birds had worked all day and the latecomers only part of the day.

Look at the parable from a contractual approach to business:

- The landowner made an agreement with his laborers based on free will. No one was forced to work. Also, the landowner was free to make his own business decisions. He was not compelled to comply with some minimum wage law or a complicated set of labor regulations.

- It was his land, so the *landowner* (get that) could do with it as he pleased. Private property ownership versus socialism's collective ownership is sharply contrasted here.

Forced redistribution of wealth is not something that God advocates. There is a strong case for this idea being rooted in envy, even if it is disguised in terms of equalizing unfairness.

Jesus loved people and did not place any store in a state welfare system, whether administered through the Roman overlords or by the Jewish religious hierarchy—the "deep state" of the day. The Jewish religious hierarchy, and King Herod, even, were corrupt and more absorbed with their own self-interests, which were rooted in envy and covetousness. They were lovers of money, not lovers of God. If this was not true, why did they not follow Jesus?

> [Pilate] knew that they had handed [Jesus] over because of envy. (Matthew 27:18)

AGENDA

> Now the Pharisees, who were lovers of money, also heard all these things, and they derided [Jesus]. (Luke 16:14)

In conclusion, Jesus always pointed those who would listen with an open heart to a personal reliance on the God of welfare, who is personally engaged with the needs of humanity everywhere and encourages personal responsibility over corporate structures.

13

DID THE EARLY CHURCH PRACTICE A FORM OF SOCIALISM?

COMMUNITY LIVING IS THE ANSWER... OR IS IT?

> *Now all who believed were together, and had all things in common, and sold their possessions and goods, and divided them among all, as anyone had need.*
> —ACTS 2:44-45

As a backdrop for this chapter, the ancient Jewish communities before Jesus' time practiced close community cooperation. Jesus and His disciples lived in a sort of communal situation for a short while (just over three years). Then the early or infant church of the book of Acts was also characterized by mutual support. However, all along private property ownership was never abandoned.

AGENDA

To be sure, the community that Jesus and His disciples enjoyed together for roughly three short years bore no resemblance to modern socialism, with its key elements of enlarging central government, control of the means of production, and so on. Their service to His cause was always voluntary—some of them even considered going back to their fishing business.

Although they shared a common purse under Judas Iscariot's corrupt control and gave to the poor from that purse, Jesus spoke more to matters of the heart when it came to money rather than setting up some sort of centralized welfare system. He was not program oriented but individual focused. Government-subsidized housing, food stamps, and unemployment benefits were *not* the order of the day.

Jesus did show His disciples that meeting people's needs through the power of God was His will. He demonstrated the heart and power of God as He fed the multitudes and healed the sick. Jesus loved people, and so must we. Serving people involves a personal response. God does not expect us to abdicate our responsibility to a distant and very often wasteful and unaccountable government agency.

WAS THE EARLY CHURCH IN THE BOOK OF ACTS SOCIALIST?

Two key passages of scripture come to mind; first, a description of the early church's activities:

DID THE EARLY CHURCH PRACTICE A FORM OF SOCIALISM?

> [The apostle Peter] testified and exhorted them, saying, "Be saved from this perverse generation." Then those who gladly received his word were baptized; and that day about three thousand souls were added to them. And they continued steadfastly in the apostles' doctrine and fellowship, in the breaking of bread, and in prayers. Then fear came upon every soul, and many wonders and signs were done through the apostles. Now all who believed were together, and had all things in common, and sold their possessions and goods, and divided them among all, as anyone had need. (Acts 2:40–47)

This passage shows the early disciples did relate communally in that they sold their goods and distributed the proceeds based on needs (v. 45). This was in the context of a great spiritual outpouring with the manifest presence of God orchestrating the hearts and actions of believers under leadership enthralled with Jesus and now with the Holy Spirit's power.

The leadership had personally paid the price of rejection and persecution from the religious establishment. They provided wholesome Bible teaching and fostered fellowship and unity around the common cause of building God's kingdom. They modeled unselfish service and were good examples of worship and witness in both word and deed. Their lives were characterized by prayer, and they often celebrated communion together. The solid foundation of their faith was Christ's death and resurrection, the pivotal, game-changing moment in human history. This was ordinary time.

AGENDA

The fruit of all these powerful spiritual dynamics was the voluntary, or freewill, giving and sharing of private property with those in need. Acts 2 does not teach a socialist sharing of the means of production or communal ownership of property, not even the forced redistribution of liquidated resources or wealth.

The second passage of note is Acts 4:32–37. The context here was that the disciples had experienced severe backlash from the threatened religious establishment. It appears as if this persecution drove the early believers closer still to God and one another.

> Now the multitude of those who believed were of one heart and one soul; neither did anyone say that any of the things he possessed was his own, but they had all things in common. And with great power the apostles gave witness to the resurrection of the Lord Jesus. And great grace was upon them all. Nor was there anyone among them who lacked; for all who were possessors of lands or houses sold them, and brought the proceeds of the things that were sold, and laid them at the apostles' feet; and they distributed to each as anyone had need.
>
> And Joses, who was also named Barnabas by the apostles (which is translated Son of Encouragement), a Levite of the country of Cyprus, having land, sold it, and brought the money and laid it at the apostles' feet.

Notice the disciples maintained private ownership but did not say that the things they possessed were their own and untouchable. In effect, they voluntarily adopted a mindset of sharing. They had been filled (refilled) with the Holy Spirit, and God's leadership was strongly present among this unified church.

The lands that were liquidated were obviously extra properties because otherwise, those who sold their land would now be in need themselves.

Fortunately, they had a tried and tested apostolic leadership living transparently before them, and the community exercised honest stewardship under God's watchful and protective eye. Acts 5 chronicles God's judgment on liars among them (Ananias and Sapphira) and shows how this process of sharing was kept real, pure, and authentic. By the way, Acts 5:4 shows that Ananias and Sapphira maintained control over the property while it was unsold, and even over the proceeds after the sale was concluded. They were free to do with their possessions as they wished. The only problem was that they were liars and had to be exposed for their deceit.

Later in the book of Acts, the early church continued to meet in homes owned by private parties. Communal ownership of property was not a feature of the early church.

> And when [Lydia] and her household were baptized, she begged us, saying, "If you have judged me to be faithful to the Lord, come to my house and stay." (Acts 16:15)

AGENDA

Love must always be the driver for any voluntary sharing or distribution of resources or wealth. When external law is enforced, it precipitates problems. The disciples themselves were the ones who determined to send relief to their needy brothers in Christ. (See Acts 11:29.) This act of kindness came from their hearts of compassion and was not imposed on them by rules from the dictatorial leadership.

The conclusion seems clear: the early church was not socialist in nature and practice.

14

KINGDOM PRINCIPLES OF *TRUE* PROSPERITY

GOD'S PLAN ALL ALONG

> *Beloved, I pray that you may prosper in all things and be in health, just as your soul prospers.*
>
> —3 JOHN 2

> *Let them shout for joy and be glad,*
> * Who favor my righteous cause;*
> *And let them say continually,*
> *"Let the LORD be magnified,*
> * Who has pleasure in the prosperity of His servant."*
>
> —PSALM 35:27

AGENDA

It is clear from God's Word that His will is for us to do well and prosper. He derives pleasure from seeing His children fulfill their destiny in a state of well-being.

True prosperity begins in the heart, or soul, at the individual level. This well-being becomes communicable in a group or collective setting as we learn to enjoy God's love for us and are motivated to serve our fellow man. Our goal no longer is to use people to get wealth, but to use wealth to help other people.

Only God can transform the human heart from one that is fearful and selfish to a servant's heart. No amount of legislation, programming, and systemic or structural change can reach down into the heart as deep as God can. Radical, lasting transformation of society starts with God's people, who are called to impact society with a lifestyle of holiness.

REDEMPTION—REPENTANCE—REBIRTH—REFORM

Public reformation of social evils always follows personal redemption and repentance (a change of mind after the truth has been presented). For example, slavery in Europe and the Americas was abolished largely because godly people were moved to confront the injustice of that evil practice. Their eyes were opened to the selfishness of that exploitation of their fellow man. The golden rule had been broken, and repentance was needed.

Sadly, today we have need of another awakening to God's gracious will and purposes for humanity. When this happens, it will involve coming to grips with the ills of modern-day slavery, whether perpetrated by sex traffickers, pedophiles, religious zealots, or economic and political slave masters.

Prosperity is not a matter of a big bank account and everything that might come from having large amounts of disposable financial resources. It is a matter of the heart: generosity, integrity, honesty, love, service—these are the stuff of prosperity.

When a people are submitted to God's purposes, they see through the false and imperfect agendas of men and give honor and glory to God as they prosper in a righteousness that "exalts a nation" (Proverbs 14:34).

> When it goes well with the righteous, the city rejoices;
> And when the wicked perish, there is jubilation.
> By the blessing of the upright the city is exalted,
> But it is overthrown by the mouth of the wicked.
> (Proverbs 11:10–11)

Our lives count. When we do well, others around us are impacted for the better. God's people, filled with His wisdom and living a life of devotion to Him and of service to their neighbors, create an environment where whole cities are blessed and where even crime rates drop.

One simply cannot set up a society with lasting success without God's help and wisdom. Every detail of our communal lives must be shaped by the principles contained in His Word.

There is no way to possibly cover the whole gamut of

principles that govern kingdom prosperity in a short chapter, so I will invite you to begin with something within your reach. Read the book of Proverbs, one chapter each day—perhaps time it with the days of the month, since there are thirty-one chapters in the book. As you absorb its truth, wisdom will be imparted to you regarding how to make a difference in everything. After all, that is what God is after: for everything to change, improve, and last.

Just do it. Come on! Your life will never be the same. Neither will your neighbor's.

15

WHY DOES ALL THIS MATTER?

AND WHAT TO DO

Righteousness exalts a nation,
But sin is a reproach to any people.

—PROVERBS 14:34

God wants any individual and nation to do well and prosper. He wants us to be in right standing with Him so that nothing stands in the way of a pure and honest relationship between Him and us. Why? So, we can hear His pertinent truth about the challenges we face. However, if we rely on our own truth and have faith in ourselves or someone else with limited resources—like the government—we will fall short of God's glory, and that is sin—a "reproach to any people."

Socialist governments seek to have a say in all aspects of life: family, child rearing, education, and churches, which are to be kept separate from impacting everyday life Monday to Saturday. In other words, "just stay in your holy huddle and focus on the sweet by and by, while we take care of the nasty here and now."

Economics, politics, communications, arts, sports, and entertainment—you name it—there is no area off-limits to their top-down regulatory control. *We (the experts) know better than you do, so put your heads down and keep working* might describe the social engineers' attitude about the business of creating a New World Order in their own image.

Yet God knows what is going on, what the globalists' agenda is. In the midst of this turmoil, He wants His people to creatively engage with the community to a much greater level and bring solutions to life's challenges without being intimidated by those with already-established agendas that mostly, if not exclusively, exclude His divine perspective.

Historically, God has used His people to lead the way in reform: Joseph in the Egyptian Pharaoh's time, Daniel in King Nebuchadnezzar's Babylonian Empire (and his successors too). Isaiah the statesman-prophet played his part in the eighth century BC speaking into the situations facing the kings of his day (Uzziah, Ahaz, and Hezekiah). In New Testament church history, even, the church has played a leading role in reforming society to conform with God's ways. A huge example is the abolition of slavery.

WHY DOES ALL THIS MATTER?

If God's people do not engage and speak into the challenges facing society, then who will? Any vacuum will be filled by people who do not know God, stumbling around in their own efforts to create "heaven on earth," their secularist utopia.

In these end times, God's people are to walk more closely in His ways and follow *His* agenda for their lives, becoming beacons of light in a dark world that always needs hope, direction, and a way out from the confusion. Hopefully, this book has helped you understand what is going on a little better and inspire you to consider your ways.

It is up to you to get together with God, through Jesus, and flesh out what part you are to play in making positive, lasting change for the better. He has given His Word, His Spirit, and His church to guide you in this process.

It has never been God's will for the church to sit on the sidelines of society on Sunday and pontificate on how bad things have gotten in the culture, and then go to work on Monday and do nothing about it, quietly trying to stay out of trouble. We are to engage, albeit with wisdom.

Jesus engaged with the culture of His day. He challenged the corrupt political and religious establishment while reaching and meeting the needs of the common citizen. Remember how He challenged the religious stranglehold of the scribes and Pharisees; how He overturned the tables of the money changers in the temple precincts; how He referred to the Jewish puppet governing authority of the day (Herod) as a sly "fox" (Luke 13:32), and even stood boldly in His moment of extreme vulnerability before Caesar's representative (Pontius Pilate) and spoke truth to power.

Jesus paved the way for His followers to stand against evil and corruption in every aspect of society. Yes, He did say that His kingdom was not of this earth (John 18:36), and that His followers were not to engage in armed insurrection ("Put up your sword, Peter," John 18:11, paraphrased). But He did focus their attention on a far greater power—the power of the Holy Spirit to change things in the human heart from within. Changed people change things. Reform follows repentance. The satanic imperial cult of the Roman Empire was changed from within as the gospel was preached and lived out in love by the likes of the apostle Paul and the second-century followers of Christ who took their stand for truth and heavenly justice.

My conviction is that everyone has a spark of genius waiting to be unwrapped. You have something to contribute to the common good, and God is waiting for you to respond to His loving promptings and discover and adopt His agenda for you.

Arise, shine; for your light has come!
And the glory of the LORD is risen upon you.
For behold, the darkness shall cover the earth,
And deep darkness the people;
But the LORD will arise over you,
And His glory will be seen upon you.
The Gentiles shall come to your light,
And kings to the brightness of your rising.

—ISAIAH 60:1–3

ADDENDUM 1

KNOW YOUR RIGHTS

THE FIRST TEN AMENDMENTS TO THE US CONSTITUTION (COMMONLY KNOWN AS THE BILL OF RIGHTS)

FIRST AMENDMENT
Congress shall make no law respecting an establishment of religion, or prohibiting the free exercise thereof; or abridging the freedom of speech, or of the press, or the right of the people peaceably to assemble, and to petition the Government for a redress of grievances.

SECOND AMENDMENT
A well regulated Militia, being necessary to the security of a free State, the right of the people to keep and bear Arms, shall not be infringed.

ADDENDUM 1

THIRD AMENDMENT
No Soldier shall, in time of peace be quartered in any house, without the consent of the Owner; nor in time of war, but in a manner to be prescribed by law.

FOURTH AMENDMENT
The right of the people to be secure in their persons, houses, papers, and effects, against unreasonable searches and seizures, shall not be violated, and no Warrants shall issue, but upon probable cause, supported by Oath or affirmation, and particularly describing the place to be searched, and the persons or things to be seized.

FIFTH AMENDMENT
No person shall be held to answer for a capital, or otherwise infamous crime, unless on a presentment or indictment of a Grand Jury, except in cases arising in the land or naval forces, or in the Militia, when in actual service in time of War or public danger; nor shall any person be subject for the same offence to be twice put in jeopardy of life or limb; nor shall be compelled in any criminal case to be a witness against himself; nor be deprived of life, liberty, or property, without due process of law; nor shall private property be taken for public use without just compensation.

SIXTH AMENDMENT
In all criminal prosecutions, the accused shall enjoy the right to a speedy and public trial, by an impartial jury of the State

and district wherein the crime shall have been committed; which district shall have been previously ascertained by law, and to be informed of the nature and cause of the accusation; to be confronted with the witnesses against him; to have compulsory process for obtaining witnesses in his favor; and to have the assistance of counsel for his defence.

SEVENTH AMENDMENT

In Suits at common law, where the value in controversy shall exceed twenty dollars, the right of trial by jury shall be preserved, and no fact tried by a jury shall be otherwise reexamined in any Court of the United States, than according to the rules of common law.

EIGHTH AMENDMENT

Excessive bail shall not be required, nor excessive fines imposed, nor cruel and unusual punishments inflicted.

NINTH AMENDMENT

The enumeration in the Constitution of certain rights shall not be construed to deny or disparage others retained by the people.

TENTH AMENDMENT

The powers not delegated to the United States by the Constitution, nor prohibited by it to the States, are reserved to the States respectively, or to the people.

ADDENDUM 2

VACCINES

BESIDES HEALTH, IS THERE AN AGENDA HERE?

No matter where you have stood on vaccines up to now, you will be forced to consider their importance in the days ahead in light of the outbreak of COVID-19 and the hurried push to develop a vaccine to counter its effects.

A *vaccine* contains an agent made from a weakened or killed form of the microbe, its toxins, or one of its surface proteins that resemble a disease-causing microorganism. The body's immune system is stimulated by the agent to recognize and destroy any microorganism associated with that agent in the future. Vaccines are thus used as prophylactics to prevent or lessen the effects of a future infection by a wild pathogen.

ADDENDUM 2

HISTORY OF VACCINES

Vaccination in some form has been practiced since at least the seventeenth century in China. Edward Jenner was the founder of Western vaccinology; in 1798 he inoculated a thirteen-year-old boy with cowpox. Louis Pasteur followed up with a vaccine for cholera and anthrax in 1897 and 1904, respectively. Since then, many vaccines have been developed against such diseases as the plague, tetanus, polio, and measles/mumps/rubella (MMR), to name a few.

Today, vaccine developers are excited about using genetic modification of RNA/DNA to produce new vaccines. Detractors are seriously concerned about scientists tampering with genes to produce vaccines with this new genetic material in it that could cascade in dangerous ways after it is injected.

Anti-vaxxers have several concerns about vaccines in general:

1. Side effects, including the sharp rise of autism (which is vigorously disputed by vaccine supporters).

According to the National Vaccine Information Center, chronic disease and disability in children has drastically increased in the past 50 years . . . In the 1990s, one child in 555 had autism, but by 2013, the figure had risen to one child in 50.[1]

---

1 Sylvia Booth Hubbard, "Are Too Many Vaccines Destroying Kids' Immune Systems?," NewsMax Health, February 5, 2015, https://www.newsmax.com/Health/Headline/vaccines-children-immune-system/2015/02/05/id/622900/.

Some argue that this has a lot to do with an increased vaccination regimen and even the use of aborted fetal tissue cell lines in the production of vaccines.

2. A distrust of Big Pharma, who may make decisions on vaccines which may not always be in the interests of consumers. Since 2011, pharmaceutical companies are no longer liable for injury and deaths caused by government-recommended and -mandated vaccines sold in the US.

3. Concern over vaccine overload. By age six, children will have had forty-nine doses of fourteen different vaccines and sixty-nine doses by the age of eighteen (CDC recommendations). Children at birth even receive a vaccine against hepatitis B, a sexually transmitted disease![2]

Anti-vaxxers are demonized as a threat to public health, even though they advocate for more humane vaccine policies that take into account the genetic and biological diversity of humans, rather than the one-size-fits-all, top-down approach that medical authorities adopt.

Authorities claim that science overwhelmingly supports vaccine safety and efficacy. Anti-vaxxers say, "Show me the science that proves the rise of autism and other neurological disorders is not due to the huge increase in vaccinations."

Some doctors argue that not enough is known about the

---

2 Hubbard.

development of a child's immune system, even saying that childhood infections help build a strong immune system in adulthood. When you artificially interfere with this development using multiple vaccines, the immune system development is harmed, opening up the adult to greater incidence of disease later. Dr David Brownstein, a board-certified family physician practicing in Michigan, had this to say about it:

> I feel that today's children, when compared to previous generations, suffer from more chronic illnesses because they are exposed to more toxins, and they are receiving too many vaccines at too young of an age. The vaccines contain toxic elements such as mercury, aluminum and formaldehyde. It is ludicrous to inject these toxic agents into our youth and expect good outcomes.

He went on to say:

> Perhaps we need to do research comparing vaccinated with non-vaccinated populations. Unbelievably, this work still has not been done. There has not been a single randomized, controlled study of a vaccinated versus a non-vaccinated population. Yet, we subject the most vulnerable of us, our children and the future of our country, to dozens of vaccines whose worth is often questionable... This is insane.[3]

---

3 Hubbard.

ADDENDUM 2

LEGISLATION TO PROTECT PHARMA COMPANIES THAT DEVELOP VACCINES

On February 23, 2011, the Supreme Court ruled that federal law prohibits lawsuits against drug makers over serious side effects from childhood vaccines. This was in the context of a National Vaccine Injury Compensation program instituted in 1986 by Congress, which protected vaccine producers from injury litigation. Congress set up this special "vaccine court" to handle claims against drug manufacturers so they would be spared the costs of constantly defending against parents' lawsuits. In this way the manufacturers would not be driven from the vaccine market.

A case of Big Brother (government) protecting the interests of Big Pharma instead of "we the people"?

THE ANNUAL FLU VACCINE

The annual flu vaccine promoted each flu season ("get your flu shot here") does not protect you against the current or latest mutated strain of the flu virus. It is anyone's guess which strains of the virus are likely to affect the population in any one season. The vaccines are developed over the course of the year, before any one season, and are thus not up-to-date.

The CDC website explains:

> The seasonal influenza (flu) vaccine is designed to protect against the three or four influenza viruses research indicates are most likely to spread and cause illness among people during the upcoming flu season. Flu viruses are constantly

ADDENDUM 2

changing, so the vaccine composition is reviewed each year and updated as needed based on which influenza viruses are making people sick, the extent to which those viruses are spreading, and how well the previous season's vaccine protects against those viruses.[4]

When it comes to statistics on the annual flu virus, it is estimated (best scientific guess)—the CDC gives no hard data on this—that from October 1, 2019, through April 4, 2020, there have been "39,000,000–56,000,000 flu illnesses," with "410,000–740,000 flu hospitalizations" and "24,000–62,000 flu deaths."[5] The numbers show quite a large range in the estimates. No accurate testing data are available.

From the CDC website again: this is how they lump the annual flu and COVID-19 incidences together:

- Laboratory-confirmed flu activity is low at this time.

- Elevated influenza-like-illness is likely related to COVID-19.[6]

---

4   Centers for Disease Prevention and Control, "Selecting Viruses for the Seasonal Influenza Vaccine," CDC website, last reviewed September 4, 2018, https://www.cdc.gov/flu/prevent/vaccine-selection.htm.

5   Centers for Disease Prevention and Control, "2019–2020 U.S. Flu Season: Preliminary Burden Estimates," CDC website, last reviewed April 17, 2020, https://www.cdc.gov/flu/about/burden/preliminary-in-season-estimates.htm.

6   Centers for Disease Prevention and Control, "Flu Season," CDC website, last reviewed June 5, 2020, https://www.cdc.gov/flu/season/index.html.

Interesting, is it not? I wonder how many COVID-19 cases were/are flu cases where no accurate testing has been forthcoming during the COVID-19 event? In the absence of clear data in this regard, remaining skeptical seems reasonable.

COVID-19 vaccine development is being fast-tracked today. The federal government introduced a Manhattan Project–style "Operation Warp Speed" in May 2020 to speed things up in the testing and trials for a new COVID-19 vaccine. The program pulls together private pharmaceutical companies, government agencies, and the military to cut development time of a vaccine by as much as eight months, with a goal of having millions of doses ready by December 2020.

Some analysts question whether the vaccine that is ultimately developed will effectively work against other mutated strains of the coronavirus in future waves of the outbreak. It appears as if they are going to push the untried RNA/DNA approach to vaccine formulation rather than the traditional approach involving a live, attenuated virus and/or dead, inactive virus in their compounds. The COVID-19 emergency has seemingly precipitated "Vaccine Generation 2.0."

VACCINES AND BILL GATES: HIS PLAN TO VACCINATE THE WORLD

Bill Gates introduced his "decade of vaccines" back in 2010, when he pledged to spend over $10 billion to advance his belief that world vaccination was imperative. He has argued that the world cannot go back to normal until all people in the world are vaccinated.

ADDENDUM 2

The Gates Foundation's enormous impact on world health authorities and national policies, even, has been the consequence of the significant funding he has supplied in strategic manner. The Gates Foundation has influence in almost all sectors of global health.

He has played a significant role in moving governments toward making promises of purchase before pharma companies have even made the products (vaccines). In this way, these companies are incentivized to go ahead, knowing they have a guaranteed market! The Coalition for Epidemic Preparedness (CEPI), signed in 2007 by leading countries such as the USA, UK, Germany, and Japan, was also sponsored by the only non-nation group: the Gates Foundation! CEPI is set to facilitate the convenient arrangement. The Gates Foundation pledged $100 million toward vaccine development to counter the COVID-19 outbreak in a recent (2020) international fund-raising drive that included world premieres and, yes, even pop artist Madonna, who donated $1 million to the Gates Foundation vaccine efforts.

Gates has also advocated for vaccine producers to be protected, or "indemnified," against the risk of individuals who have been hurt by vaccines suing developers and manufacturers.[7] To this end, the US Department of Health and Human Services has already been working on a plan to indemnify developers, manufacturers, distributors, and

---

[7] See the four-part series on Bill Gates and his foundation at https://www.youtube.com/watch?v=8alro6mjcsU.

medical personnel workers in this field. This plan was set out on March 17, 2020, retroactive to February 4, 2020.

Incidentally, during the "decade of vaccines" (2010–2020), Bill Gates's personal net worth has grown from $45 billion to $100 billion. Despite giving away billions to philanthropy through the Bill & Melinda Gates Foundation, and selling much of his Microsoft stock, he has reinvested in various sectors, including pharmaceuticals.

BIG MEDIA AND CORPORATE INFLUENCE

Bill Gates and his foundation generally receive good press, at least from big media outlets. He has made sizable donations to a host of mainstream corporate media outlets. The *Guardian* newspaper, NBC Universal, the influential French newspaper *Le Monde*, NPR, and Al-Jazeera have all received millions of dollars from the Gates Foundation. An astonishing $49 million was given to the BBC's Media Action program. MSNBC stands for Microsoft NBC. He who pays the piper calls the tune.

Big Pharma has influence over mass media outlets, which have been united in attacking parents and physicians who defend the ethical principle of informed consent to vaccination. These outlets are also calling for vaccine exemptions based on religious grounds for example, to be severely restricted or eliminated.

Apple, Google, Microsoft, Amazon, and Facebook dominate online communications and sales. They are positioned to join together to aggressively market vaccines and promote a "no exceptions" vaccine policy endorsed by the WHO (World Health Organization) and many governments worldwide. YouTube (under Google) has even stated they will censor "harmful" or "problematic" conversations about vaccination and health.[8]

VACCINES, THE NEW WORLD ORDER, AND SOCIALISM

The WHO is the world's largest and most influential public health agency. The Gates Foundation is the largest non-state funder of the WHO since 1998 and is the second-largest WHO funder overall (after the US government, which, under Trump, is pulling its funding from WHO due to bias toward China). This foundation significantly influences the setting of the WHO's program priorities, including vaccine production marketing and implementation.

The world's five largest pharmaceutical companies—Pfizer, Roche, Johnson & Johnson, SANOFI, and Merck—are ready to produce and promote vaccinations throughout the world.

---

8   Andrew Hutchinson, "YouTube Ramps Up Action to Remove COVID-19 Misinformation," SocialMediaToday, April 23, 2020, https://www.socialmediatoday.com/news/youtube-ramps-up-action-to-remove-covid-19-misinformation/576577/; CNN, "Inside YouTube's 'Numerous Policy Changes' during the Pandemic," CNN Business, 2020, https://edition.cnn.com/videos/business/2020/04/19/inside-youtubes-numerous-policy-changes-during-the-pandemic.cnn.

ADDENDUM 2

A New World Order of top-down control by centralized authorities and governments is being facilitated through medical means as one of its central pillars. The COVID-19 pandemic could well be used to advance their agenda.

ADDENDUM 3

WHO ARE "THEY"?

GLOBALIST WORLD INFLUENCERS AND THEIR SOCIALIST COHORTS (A SAMPLING DRAWN FROM THEIR WEBSITES)

NOTE: *The "face" of these organizations as presented on their websites seems well and good. However, when you dig deeper the agenda behind the agenda becomes clearer. Sometimes it is hidden in plain sight, and sometimes not.*

BILDERBERG GROUP
"*The annual Bilderberg Meeting is a three-day forum for informal discussions, designed to foster dialogue between Europe and North America.*" (https://bilderbergmeetings.org/background/brief-history)

ADDENDUM 3

WORLD ECONOMIC FORUM.
"The World Economic Forum is the International Organization for Public-Private Cooperation.

"The Forum engages the foremost political, business, cultural and other leaders of society to shape global, regional and industry agendas." (https://www.weforum.org/about/world-economic-forum)

COUNCIL ON FOREIGN RELATIONS
FOUNDED ON JULY 29, 1921
"We shall have world government whether or not you like it—by conquest or consent." (CFR member James Warburg, speaking before the U.S. Congress, February 1950)

BILL GATES AND THE BILL &
MELINDA GATES FOUNDATION
"All lives have equal value. We are impatient optimists working to reduce inequality." (https://www.gatesfoundation.org/)

THE UNITED NATIONS
"Peace, dignity and equality on a healthy planet." (https://www.un.org/en/)

GEORGE SOROS AND THE OPEN
SOCIETY FOUNDATIONS
"The Open Society Foundations work to build vibrant and inclusive democracies whose governments are accountable to their citizens." (https://www.opensocietyfoundations.org/)

ADDENDUM 3

MARK ZUCKERBERG AND THE CHAN ZUCKERBERG INITIATIVE
"Our mission is to find new ways to leverage technology, community-driven solutions, and collaboration to accelerate progress in Science, Education, and within our Justice & Opportunity work." (https://chanzuckerberg.com/)

THE INTERNATIONAL MONETARY FUND
"The IMF was conceived in July 1944 at the United Nations Bretton Woods Conference in New Hampshire, United States. The 44 countries in attendance sought to build a framework for international economic cooperation and avoid repeating the competitive currency devaluations that contributed to the Great Depression of the 1930s. The IMF's primary mission is to ensure the stability of the international monetary system—the system of exchange rates and international payments that enables countries and their citizens to transact with each other." (https://www.imf.org/en/About/Factsheets/IMF-at-a-Glance)

THE WORLD BANK
"With 189 member countries, staff from more than 170 countries, and offices in over 130 locations, the World Bank Group is a unique global partnership: five institutions working for sustainable solutions that reduce poverty and build shared prosperity in developing countries." (https://www.worldbank.org/)

ADDENDUM 3

ROYAL INSTITUTE OF INTERNATIONAL AFFAIRS (RIIA)

"Chatham House, the Royal Institute of International Affairs, is independent and owes no allegiance to any government or to any political body. It does not take institutional positions on policy issues.

"As a world-leading policy institute, our mission is to help governments and societies build a sustainably secure, prosperous and just world." (https://www.chathamhouse.org/about)

TRILATERAL COMMISSION

"The Trilateral Commission is a non-governmental, policy-oriented forum that brings together leaders in their individual capacity from the worlds of business, government, academia, press and media, as well as civil society. The Commission offers a global platform for open dialogue, reaching out to those with different views and engaging with decision makers from around the world with the aim of finding solutions to the great geopolitical, economic and social challenges of our time." (http://trilateral.org/)

ROCKEFELLER FOUNDATION

"The Foundation is focused on four core commitments: to end energy poverty, achieve health for all, nourish the world, and expand economic opportunity. We are pursuing these goals through innovative partnerships and through impact investments that find new ways to leverage private capital for social good." (https://www.rockefellerfoundation.org/about-us/our-history/)

ADDENDUM 3

CLUB OF ROME

"The Club of Rome was created to address the multiple crises facing humanity and the planet. Drawing on the unique, collective know-how of our 100 members—notable scientists, economists, business leaders and former politicians—we seek to define comprehensive solutions to the complex, interconnected challenges of our world.

"Decades of exponential consumption and population growth have come to imperil the earth's climate and life-supporting systems, while reinforcing social and economic inequalities and impoverishing billions globally.

"As a network of thought leaders from a rich diversity of expertise, our members are committed to facilitating the difficult conversations and the bold actions required to confront the planetary emergency facing humanity and our common home. Our goal is to actively advocate for paradigm and systems shifts which will enable society to emerge from our current crises, by promoting a new way of being human, within a more resilient biosphere." (https://clubofrome.org/about-us/)

ABOUT THE AUTHOR

Ed was born and raised in South Africa, played state-level rugby, graduated with honors from university, received Jesus in 1979, and came with his family to the United States in April 1994 to play his part in helping equip the body of Christ with the Word of God. His wonderful wife's name is Sue, and they have three grown children, all serving God: Janine, Matthew (married to Angela), and Benjamin.

Ed attended Bible school in 1980 and helped build a large revival church ministry that flourished in times of great political and social upheaval in the nation.

Ed has served full-time in ministry since 1981, first as a youth pastor, then later as Bible school instructor, associate pastor, school principal, church planter, and Bible school dean.

Since 1994, Ed has served the Lord from our base in the United States, ministering also in Africa, Europe, England, Scotland, Wales, and Australia.

ABOUT THE AUTHOR

Ed pioneered a church as senior pastor in Washington State from 1999, returning to California in 2005 to continue ministering in the local church and the body of Christ. He then pioneered another church in Washington State from 2010 on.

He continues to equip the church through a variety of media resources.

Ed's practical message of power, and change has helped many fulfill their end-time mandate to reach and disciple the lost.

WWW.EDHORAK.COM